Patient waiting for the earth to bloom develops a little child spiritually.

MONTESSORI CHILDREN

BY

CAROLYN SHERWIN BAILEY

NEW YORK
HENRY HOLT AND COMPANY
1915

MONTESSORI CHILDREN

BY

CAROLYN SHERWIN BAILEY

ILLUSTRATED FROM SPECIALLY POSED PHOTOGRAPHS

NEW YORK
HENRY HOLT AND COMPANY
1915

THE QUINN & BODEN CO. PRESS
RAHWAY, N. J.

PREFACE

As a student of child psychology and always most deeply interested in the welfare problems that confront us in connection with the upbringing of little children, I went to Rome in 1913 to study, first-hand, the results of the Montessori system of education. A great deal had been written and said in connection with the technic of the system. Little had been given the world in regard to individual children who were developing their personalities through the auto-education of Montessori. I wished to observe Montessori children.

Through the gracious courtesy of Dr. Montessori, I was given the privilege of observing in the new Trionfale School where the method could be watched from its inception, and in the Fua Famagosta and Franciscan Convent Schools. I was also given the privilege of hearing Dr. Montessori lecture, elucidating certain problems in her theory of education not previously given publicity.

I found little ones of three, four, and five years,

surrounded by the many observers of the first international Montessori training class, yet so marvelously poised and self-controlled that they went through the days as if alone. I saw such proofs of the integrity of the system as the instances of Otello, Bruno, and others.

The pages which follow constitute a series of pictures of real child types showing Montessori results. As a record of results, I hope they may contribute to the world's greater faith in the discovery of Montessori—the spirit of the child.

CAROLYN SHERWIN BAILEY.

NEW YORK, 1915.

CONTENTS

v

ILLUSTRATIONS

MONTESSORI CHILDREN

DR. MONTESSORI, THE WOMAN

A HOLIDAY in Rome, the Eternally Old, the Eternally Young. A long, sun-dried street that flanks the Tiber is gay with fruit venders who push along their carts of gold oranges, strings of dates, and amber lemons. Italians of the wealthy class mingle in friendly fashion with the native-costumed peasants. Someone starts a snatch of song; a dozen passersby take up the strain. Where the chariots of the Cæsars rattled by in yesterday's centuries, there rises a stately row of stucco apartment mansions with terraced gardens where pink roses and purple heliotrope run riot over the hedges and silver-toned fountains sing, all day long, their tinkling tunes.

Leaving the gay, bright street, you ring the electric bell at number 5 Principessa Clotilde.

"Is the Dottoressa at home, or is she keeping holiday, too?" you ask of the porter. He laughs, motioning you to an almost human elevator that lifts itself and will stop at whichever floor you ask it.

" Yes, La Dottoressa Montessori is in—in fact, she is nearly always in because of the many people, mainly Americans, who come to see her. And the children come daily to see her as well." The porter shrugs his shoulders, uncomprehendingly, as you enter the elevator and stop at the fourth floor. The popularity of this tenant of his is a matter of wonder to the porter.

As a low-voiced maid opens a great carved door and you find yourself in Dr. Montessori's apartment, you hold your breath at the modernism of it. Plain white woodwork, fine old rugs covering the stone floors, the soft tan walls covered with a few beautiful tapestries; French furniture and electric lights. The reception room in which you wait might be that of an American home, but a glance out of the open window unfolds to you the heart of the tenant. While her home is in one of the most beautiful and cultured centers of Rome, Dr. Montessori sees daily a tiny, narrow Roman alleyway where the " people " live like bees in a hive and the doorsills throng with little children and their voices rise to her every hour of the day.

But you hear a step. You turn. You are face to face with Maria Montessori.

At first you have no words. You have seen her picture in America, but it gave you no conception of the fine, chiseled beauty of the woman who stands before you dressed in severe black that accentuates the marble of the classic features, the depth of the far-seeing, dark eyes. Poise, grace, self-control, sympathy, love of humanity are written on the face. It is as if all the Madonnas of the imagination of the old Italian painters had come to life in La Dottoressa. Overpowering the first glance of courteous welcome, though, that accompanied her outstretched hand is a look of stern query.

Why have you come? Are you another of the curious visitors who have besieged her from almost every nation the past year to try and grasp in a day her method of teaching that she gained only through twenty years of patient, tireless scientific study of the child mind, she seems to ask. But your words come like a torrent now. You assure her that you have made this pilgrimage to Rome, not as an individual, but as the voice of thousands of mothers who have children to be educated. They ask Dr. Montessori, through you, for her message to the American people. As you linger

over the words, *madre*, mother, and *bambino*, baby,
Dr. Montessori smiles. You have set her doubts
at rest. She talks fast, eloquently, in her musical
Italian, and you listen, thrilled, fascinated. Often
you are interrupted, but always by children.
Lovely, dark-eyed, courteous little Roman boys
and girls they are. They come from you know
not where, are admitted to Dr. Montessori's apartment quite as if they were adult visitors, and after
they have greeted her in their graceful, polite
fashion, they quietly run about the room or sit in
groups talking together as if the apartment were
the popular meeting place for all the children of
the neighborhood. You find their interruption
and their presence a help instead of a hindrance
to your interview. They illustrate by their loving
friendship for La Dottoressa and each other, and
by their complete self-control, the message that
Dr. Montessori gives you to carry back to the
American people.

She would liberate the children.

*The American people are free, but American
children are not.*

We have lost sight of the Republic of Childhood, she says. Through forcing our adult

standards of conduct and teaching upon children, we have closed the gateways of their souls. We must believe that every child, well-born into the world, is going to be good and happy and intelligent if we as parents and teachers give him a fair chance. We must stop *commanding* our children. Instead, we will *lead* them.

Dr. Montessori tells us that we are undergoing a slow but certain change in the social structure of society. Woman is being emancipated from her domestic slavery of yesterday. We are creating a new and more healthful environment for the laboring man. But the American child is still a slave to the capricious commands of his parents, which claim his soul and prevent his free, natural development to his best manhood. In school, too, children are still bound.

The vertebral column, Dr. Montessori tells us, which is biologically the most fundamental part of the human skeleton; which survived the desperate struggles of primitive man against the beasts of the desert, helped him to quarry out a shelter for himself from the solid rock and bend iron to his uses, cannot resist the bondages of the present-day *school desk*. Curvature of the spine is alarmingly prevalent among children and is increasing. Instead of resorting to surgical methods, corsets, braces, and orthopædic means for straightening child bodies, we should try to bring about some more rational method of teaching that children shall no longer be obliged to remain for the greater part of the day in such a pathologically dangerous position.

Not only do we hurt child bodies by the confinement of the school desk, but we wound their souls by ever offering rewards and punishments, by insisting upon such long periods of absolute silence as are demanded in our schools, and by imposing upon children a program of instruction that is built, often by law, to be followed by large groups of children. The normal child is he who finds it impossible to follow a program of school work or to obey, unquestioningly, the arbitrary commands of his parents. He must follow his own bent, providing he does not interfere with the freedom of others, if he is to dig out his own life path. The abnormal child is the one who *never resists;* he is the child who, without dissent, obeys all adult commands.

So Dr. Montessori, who has discovered a method of free teaching by means of which children from two and a half to five develop naturally and happily along lines that culminate in a spontaneous " explosion " into self-taught reading and writing at four and five years, speaks to the American parent.

She begs us to give our children the freedom that is the American nation's boast. Not the freedom that would lead to disordered acts, but that liberty which means the untrammeled exercise of all the moral and intellectual powers that are born with the individual.

About twenty years ago Maria Montessori, a beautiful young society girl of Rome, startled Italy by receiving with honors her degree as Doctor of Medicine. The Italian girl of the cultured classes is essentially a home girl. She studies at home, she embroiders, she plays with flowers, she is introduced to society—then she marries. That Maria Montessori should desert the quiet, rose-strewn paths of Roman débutantes and, after taking her degree, act as assistant doctor in the Psychiatric Clinic of the University of Rome, startled all Italy.

Her work at the clinic led her to visit the general insane asylums, and she became deeply interested in the deficient children who were housed there, with no attempts being made to educate them. As she studied these helpless little ones, the idea came to her that it might be possible, by putting them into better surroundings, and giving them opportunity for free gymnastic activities and free use of the senses, to educate them. She gave up medicine for teaching and again startled Italy—and the world. Her deficient children learned to read and write, easily and naturally, and took their places beside normal children in the municipal schools.

Then Dr. Montessori carried her method of physical and sense education a lap farther. If this method stimulated to action the sleeping mind of a deficient child, might it not save time and energy in the teaching of normal children, she asked herself. At that time, the Good Building Association of Rome was tearing down the squalid, disease-filled houses of the poor of the San Lorenzo Quarter and putting up in their places hygienic model tenements. Dr. Montessori arranged to have the children of each tenement gathered in one room of the basement, where large, free spaces, didactic apparatus, hot meals, and gardens would make it a Children's House. She applied her method in numerous of these Children's Houses and in the beautiful convent of the Franciscan nuns on the Via Giusti.

Again the miracle happened. Children of four began to read and write, having taught themselves. There were other wonders, too. These Montessori-trained children were self-controlled, free, happy, good. To-day there are Montessori mothers all over the world.

To furnish the right environment for the expanding of the child soul, Dr. Montessori urges that every home be transformed into a House of Childhood. It will not consist alone of walls, she tells us, although these walls will be the bulwarks of the sacred intimacy of the family. The home will be more than this. It will have a soul, and will embrace its inmates with the consoling arms of love. The new mother will be liberated, like the butterfly bursting its winter cocoon of imprisonment and darkness, from those drudgeries that the home has demanded of her in the past, leaving her better able to bear strong children, study those children, teach them, and be a social force in the world.

The new father will cultivate his health, guard his virtue, that he may better the species and make his children better, more perfect, and stronger than any which have been created before.

The ideal home of to-morrow will be the home of those men and women who wish to improve the human species and send the race on its triumphant way into eternity.

So Dr. Montessori, physician, psychologist, teacher, lover of children, and womanly woman, speaks to us.

As one says *addio* and leaves her and goes down into the blue, star-filled evening of the Eternal City, the night seems to be charged with a new mystery. Rome, who holds in her beautiful hands such good gifts for us—art, sculpture, history, painting—now offers to us another. Stretching farther than the moss-grown stones that line the Appian Way, she shows us a new road—the way that leads to the soul of a little child.

WITH MARGHERITA IN THE CHIL-
DREN'S HOUSE

*Showing the Unconscious Influence of the True
Montessori Environment*

It is so early in the sweet, perfume-laden Italian
morning that the dew is still hanging in diamond
drops on the iris and roses in the garden of the
Casa dei Bambini of the Via Giusti, Rome. The
great white room, with its flooding sunlight and
host of tiny, waiting chairs and tables, is empty,
quiet, calm.

Margherita stands a happy second in the wide-
arched doorway that makes room and garden melt
into one fragrant, peaceful whole. A wee four-
year-old girlie is Margherita, big-eyed, radiant
with smiles, and tugging a huge wicker basket of
lunch that is almost as large as she. She is the
first baby to arrive at the Children's House. Ah,
but that does not ruffle her composure. She is
already alone in her newly-found freedom of spirit.
She needs no teacher.

She places the lunch basket on a waiting bench, crosses to a wall space where rows of diminutive pink and blue aprons hang at comfortable reaching distances for little arms. She finds her own apron, wriggles into it, *buttons* it at the back. She is ready for the day.

What shall come first in Margherita's day? So much is in store for her, waiting for her eager finger tips, her electric-charged soul. As her great brown eyes slowly trail the room and the colorful garden outside, it is as if she were making a soul search for that " good thing " which will be her first silent teacher. Her glance lingers on the terraced rows of flowers, the tinkling fountain in the center. She has found the object of her search. She runs—no, she *floats*, for such complete physical control of her limbs has this four-year-old baby—to the garden, and kneels there, looking up at a redolent, yellow rose that has opened in the night. She does not touch it; she only looks and breathes and wonders. She has watched for this unfolding daily, waiting with sweet patience for the branch to burst into bud and the bud to unfold into bloom. She has tugged a vase of water each morning to offer drink to the roots. Now her patience and her service are rewarded. As she kneels there looking up into the petals of the gold flower, her small hands clasped over her breast with devotional ecstasy, *Nature opens her heart to the heart of a little child.*

Many rapturous minutes the baby kneels. Then she flies back to the room again and glances at it with the critical eye of a housekeeper. Here she flicks away a speck of dust, there she picks up a scrap of paper from the stone floor. She peeps into the wall cabinets that hold the Montessori didactic materials to see if the gay buttoning, lacing, and bow-tying frames, the fascinating pink blocks of the tower, the frames of form insets are all in their places. In the meantime the Signorina directress comes. Bruno, of five, arrives, bringing with him his two-and-a-half-year-old brother. More toddlers trail in, two and a half, three, four, four and a half years old, and button themselves into their pink and blue aprons. Independent, polite, joyous little children of the Cæsars they are, each with his or her own special happy task in mind in coming to the Children's House this blue day.

The wee-est toddlers drag out soft-colored rugs,

orange, dull green, deep crimson, and spread them
on the wide white spaces of the sun-flecked stone
floor. Here they build and rebuild the enchanting
intricacies of the tower of blocks, the broad stair
of blocks, and the red and white rods of the long
stair, chanting to themselves as they unconsciously
measure distances and make mental comparisons:
" big, little; thick, thin; long, short."

Children of three and a half and four take from
the cabinets boxes of many-colored, silk-wound
spools, which they sort and lay upon the little
tables in chromatic order until a rainbow-tinted
mass lies before their pigment-loving eyes. From
the bright scarlet of poppies to the faint blush of
pale pink coral, from the royal purple of the tall,
spiked Roman iris to the amethyst tint of a wild
orchid, they make no mistake in the intermediate
color gradations. Other children of four and
over finger with intelligent, trained skill the geometric forms; circles, triangles, squares that they
are learning to recognize through the " eyes in
their fingers," and which will help them to see
with the mind's eye the form that makes the beauty
of our world. Small Joanina, in her corner, runs
her forefinger with the greatest delicacy of touch

a dozen times around a circle. Then she fits it in
its place in the form board, takes it out and fits it
in again. Then she looks up, a new light in her
eyes, darts out into the garden and walks slowly
about the fountain, running her finger around its
deep basin.

"Signorina, Signorina!" she calls. "The
fountain is a circle. I can see a pebble that is a
circle, too. I see *many* circles!"

So the children learn through the *exercise of the
senses*.

But Margherita?

All this time she has flitted from one task to
another. She found an outlined picture of clover
leaves and colored it with dainty pencil strokes,
making the leaves deep green and the background
paler, and handling her pencil with careful skill.
Then she took a box of white cards on which
are mounted great black letters, cut from fine
sandpaper. Holding each card in her left hand,
she traced the form of the letter with her right
forefinger, closed her eyes, traced its form again,
repeated the letter's name to herself in a whisper,
sat silently a second.

As the Signorina directress moves from child

to child, smiling encouragement, showing Bruno's baby brother's clumsy fingers how to slip a button through a buttonhole, helping Joanina to find a new form, the square, she watches Margherita.

"This may be a white day in the child's mind growth," she thinks, but she does not suggest, or hurry the miracle. She only waits, hopes, watches.

Silence is written on the blackboard. Three hours have passed in which over thirty children, barely out of babyhood, have worked incessantly at many different occupations, have moved gracefully and with complete freedom about the room, have changed occupations as often as they wished, have not once quarreled. But now, out of the ordered disorder, comes a marvelous hush. No word is spoken, but one baby after another, glancing the written sign, drops back with closed eyes into a hushed silence in which the whir of bird wings in the garden, the fluttering of casement hangings, the far-away sound of a bell are audible. Even Bruno's baby brother struggles not to make a clattering noise with his little chair. No one has said to this two-year-old, "Be still." Rather, has he been inspired to *feel* stillness.

Out of the restful calm of the room comes the

whispered call of the Signorina: " Bruno, Piccola, Maria, Joanina, Margherita!" Lightly, noiselessly, joyously the children come and huddle in a hushed group about the directress. She has called to the soul of each child, she has commended them for their self-taught lesson in control.

As the work with the didactic materials is taken up again, Margherita sits in a little chair for a space, quiet, reflective. Her lips move, her fingers trace signs in the air and on the table before her. The Game of Silence has helped this four-year-old with her spirit unfolding. Now, with a sudden impulse, she darts to the blackboard, seizes a piece of chalk, *writes*.

" Ma-ma! Ma-ma! "

Margherita writes it a dozen times in clear, flowing script with breathless, eager strokes.

" Signorina, Signorina, I write—I write about my mother. I *write!* " she joyously interpolates.

The other children look up with sympathetic interest, some leaving their work to crowd about the victorious Margherita. All of them voice their sympathy.

" Margherita writes," they say. With the older ones who have already reached this wonder lap in their education there is a note of *nonchalance*.

"We also write," they seem to say. With the tiny ones there is a note of hopeful promise.

"Some day we, too, will find that we can write," they seem to say.

Margherita covers the blackboard with clear, big script. She erases it all for the sheer joy of assuring herself that she is able to write it all over again. When the luncheon hour comes, she looks back longingly at the blackboard as she lays plates on the little tables with dainty precision, places knife, fork, and spoon deftly, carries five tumblers at a time on a tray without dropping one, and passes a tureen of hot soup that is so large as to almost hide her small self. Even the happiness of being one of such a happy "party," of eating one's lunch of peas and sweet wheat bread and soup in the Children's House, does not wholly satisfy Margherita to-day. Her big brown eyes are raised continually to her first written word.

Luncheon over, the children, with balls, hoops, and toys, romp out for an hour's play in the garden.

"Margherita," Bruno calls. "Come, we will have The Little One for a donkey, and I will harness him with you, who may be the horse!"

But the little girl, usually the first to start a game, does not hear. She is seated under the rosebush as if she were telling *her* rose the wonder that has come to her to-day. She and the rose have unfolded together. So it is with all Montessori children. They open their souls as flowers do, naturally, freely, surely.

Margherita is your child as well as the precious *bambino* of her Roman mother. Children the world over, from sun to sun, from pole to pole, are the same in these plastic first years of mind growth. They have the same insatiable desire to *do*, to *touch*, to be *free in activity*. Not always understanding the little child's hereditary way of grasping knowledge, we wound his spirit by crushing these natural instincts. We say, "*don't touch*," "*be still*," because the activities of our small Margheritas and Brunos interfere with our adult standards of living.

Dr. Montessori has discovered that to say, "*don't touch*," "*be still*," to a child is a crime.

Such commands are the keen-edged daggers that kill the child soul.

It is possible that some time will elapse before Dr. Montessori's system of setting the clockwork of the little child's mind running automatically, of opening the floodgates of the child soul can be adopted in their entirety in our American school. We are so used to thinking of a school as a crowded place of many desks, where children must remain, bound physically and mentally by the will of the teacher and the relentless course of study, that a Montessori schoolroom where, as Dr. Montessori herself expresses it, children may move about usefully, intelligently, and freely, without committing a rough or rude act, seems to us impossible. We even prescribe and teach imaginative *plays* to our children—as if it were possible for any outside force to mold that wonderful mind force by means of which the mind creates the *new* out of its triumphant conquest of the world through the senses.

Ideal Montessori schools may be our hope of tomorrow, but to make of a home a Children's House is the fact of to-day.

To bring about Montessori development in the

home is not alone a matter of buying the didactic materials and then offering them to your Margherita and looking for their future miracle working. This would mean stimulating lawlessness instead of freedom. Many of our children already play with squares and circles without seeing how squares and circles make beauty in the architecture of our cities. Many of our children grow up side by side with opening roses without unfolding with them. We would most of us rather button on our babies' aprons, tie their bibs, feed them, than lead them into the physical independence that comes from doing these things themselves. We wish children to be obedient, but instead of establishing principles of good in their minds which they will follow freely, if we only give them a chance, we *command*, and expect unreasoning obedience to our injustice.

A Children's House in every home will be a place where the mother is imbued with the spirit of the investigator. She watches her children, asking herself why they act along certain lines. She leads instead of ruling. She will teach her children physical independence as soon as they can toddle. To know how to dress and undress, to bathe, to look quickly over a room to see if it is in order, to open and close doors and move little chairs, tables, and toys quietly, to care for plants and pets—these are simple physical exercises which help to keep children free and good. She will provide her Children's House with materials for sense-training. She will lead her children by simple, logical steps into preparation for early mastery of reading and writing.

The first step, however, in giving the American child a chance to develop along the self-active, natural lines of Margherita is to fill our homes with the spirit of Montessori. We will have unlimited patience with the mistakes and idiosyncrasies of childhood, remembering that we do not aim to develop little men and women but only as nearly perfect children as we can. We will endeavor to surround ourselves with those influences of love and charity and beauty and simplicity which it will be good for our children to feel as well. We will offer the children the best food, the greatest amount of air, the brightest sunshine, the least breakable belongings, the most encouragement, the minimum of coercion.

Our attitude toward the child will be that of

the physician to whom the slightest variation of a
symptom is a signal for a change of treatment, to
whom a fraction of progress measures a span. A
careful home record of the child's mental, moral,
and physical gain should be kept, and it will be
radiantly discovered that the removal of the burden of force and coercion from the shoulders of
the little child will give him an impetus, not only
to mind growth, but to the attaining of greater
bodily strength.

Much misunderstanding of the system of Montessori has come about through our too lavish in-
terpretation of the word *freedom* as lawlessness.
It should be interpreted, rather, as *self-direction*.
The home in which the children are provided with
good living conditions, in which it is made possible for them to grow naturally, where their longing to see and touch and weigh and smell and taste
is satisfied as far as can be arranged, and where
they are led to be as independent of adult help
as possible, is laying the foundation for the education of Montessori.

VALIA

The Physical Education of the System

VALIA was her mother's little stranger. Although the mother had borne and fondled and bathed and clothed and undressed the pink flesh that held the baby soul, she did not know that flesh. And Valia grew to be three years old, fat and good, but with little bent limbs and a tired-out spine and clumsy, fumbling fingers.

"Sit in your chair, Valia. That is what chairs are made for," Valia's mother admonished at home when the baby joyfully pranced across the floor on "all fours" or lay prone at play with her toys.

"Walk in the garden path like a little lady," she urged, when Valia, taken out for a walk, climbed to the lowest railing of an adjacent fence and walked along it, sideways, or hung from the top, her fat legs swinging in the air.

"Do not jump; to jump is noisy and unbecoming in little girls," the mother commanded, as Valia, brought to the Trionfale Children's House in Rome, hopped gayly up and down the wide stone steps.

But the directress of the school had no word of reproof for baby Valia. She looked at the bent legs that could hardly hold the weight of the plump body, she glanced at the powerless baby hands that could not clutch with any force the handles of a toy wheelbarrow which another child offered Valia for her play.

" You have not noticed the baby's limbs," the directress suggested.

The mother's eyes trailed the school yard where Valia struggled to keep up with the other sturdy little men and women who trundled their toy wheelbarrows up and down in long happy lines. She shrugged her shoulders.

" Perhaps they are crooked, but what can one do to the body of a *bambino* but feed and cover it? " she asked in discouraged query.

" Ah, La Dottoressa tells us," the directress replied simply.

"We can *know the body* of the little child."

The education of Valia's muscles was begun that very day, that instant.

In the school garden the little maid found her way with the other children to an immediately fascinating bit of gymnastic apparatus; a section of a low fence it looked, its posts sunk deeply into the ground so as to make it strong and durable. It was the right height for small arms to reach the top rail, which was round, smooth, and easily grasped by small hands. Here Valia hung, her limbs suspended and at rest, for long periods. Sometimes she pulled her body up so that her waist was level with the upper railing. It was a new game, one could climb a fence without being chided for it. Valia did not know, but Dr. Montessori did, that little children climb fences, pull back when we lead them, and try to draw themselves up by clinging to furniture because they need this form of physical exercise to bring about harmonious muscular development. Valia's body was developing at an enormously greater rate than her limbs. The height of your baby's torso at one year is about sixty-five per cent. of its total stature, at two years is sixty-three per cent., at three years is sixty-two per cent. But the limbs

Back-yard apparatus for the physical development of children is valuable.

of the baby, ah, these develop much more slowly. To hang from the top railing of a fence straightens the spine, rests the short limbs by removing the weight of the torso, and helps the hands to prehensive grasping. So Dr. Montessori invented and uses this bar apparatus with the children at Rome and recommends its use in American nurseries and playrooms.

The next Montessori exercise for Valia was a simple, rhythmic one—walking on a line to secure bodily poise and limb control.

It was just another game for a child, full of happy surprise, too, for she never knew when the sweet notes of the piano in the big rooms of the Children's House would tinkle out their call to the march. But when the pianist played a tune that was simple and repeated its melody over and over again and was marked in its rhythm, Valia and Otello and Mario and all the other babies put away their work and fluttered like wind-blown butterflies over to the place where a big circle was outlined in white paint on the floor. To march upon this line, now fast, now slowly, sometimes with the lightness of a fairy and then with the joyously loud tramp of a work horse, oh, how delightful! Sometimes the music changed to the rhythm of running or a folk-dance step, and this gave further delight to the little ones.

At first, Valia could not find the white circle of delight. Her fat feet refused to obey the impulse of her eagerly musical soul. But with the days she found poise and grace and erectness and the crooked limbs began to straighten themselves.

She sat, for hours at a time, in a patch of sunlight on the floor, using her incompetent little fingers in some of the practical exercises of everyday living. The directress gave her a stout wooden frame, to which were fastened two soft pieces of gay woolen stuff, one of which was pierced with buttonholes and the other having large bone buttons. Valia worked all one morning before she was able to fit each button in its corresponding buttonhole, but when she did accomplish this, the triumph was a bit of wonder-working in Valia's control of herself. It started her on the road to physical freedom.

Happy in her new accomplishment, she mastered all the other dressing frames; the soft linen with pearl buttons that was like her underlinen, the leather through which one thrust shoe buttons

An important physical exercise of Montessori.

with one's own button hook, or laced from one eye-let to another, the lacing on cloth like her mother's Sunday bodice of green velvet, the frames of linen with large and small hooks and eyes, the frame upon which were broad strands of bright-colored ribbon to be tied in a row of smart little bows.

Daily, simple physical exercises such as these; hand and eye co-ordination, exercises in poise, stretching, rest for the limbs and freedom for the spine and torso slowly transformed Valia from a lump of disorganized, putty-like flesh to an erect, graceful, self-controlled little woman.

"What have you done to my Valia?" asked the mother as she waited at the school door for her little one a few months later. "She dresses the young *bambino* at home and buttons her own shoes. She no longer stumbles all day long but stands well on her feet. She helps me to lay the evening meal and carries a dish of soup, full, to the place of her father. I do not understand it. Did you punish her for climbing and being clumsy?"

"No." The directress of the Children's House lays a kind hand on Valia's curly head as she explains. "We did not punish Valia. We gave her a fence upon which to climb and we let her tumble about on the floor when she was tired, and we helped her to find her feet and her fingers."

Dr. Montessori tells us that there is a little Valia in every home. The child from one to three and four years of age is in need of definite physical exercises that will tend to the normal development of physiological movements. We ordinarily give the little child's body slight thought. Then, in the schools, we gather older children into large classes, and by a series of collective gymnastics in which the commands of the teacher check all spontaneity, we try to secure poise and self-control and grace for the child body.

Gymnastics for the home will accomplish this result, Dr. Montessori tells us, and these include simple exercises such as one sees in the Children's Houses. They are planned taking into account the biology of the body of the child from birth to six years of age—the child who has a torso greatly developed in comparison with his lower limbs. They have for their basis these goals:

Helping the child to limb development and control.

Hand and eye work in connection in exercises
of practical life.

Helping the child to proper breathing and articulate speech.

Helping the child to achieving the practical acts of life; dressing, carrying objects without dropping, and the resulting co-ordination of hand and eye.

To bring about this physical development, Dr. Montessori has planned and put into the Children's Houses in Rome certain very simple physical exercises, so simple as to seem to us almost obvious, but the results in child poise, control, and grace have drawn the attention of the entire world. These exercises include:

Swinging and " chinning " on a play fence, modeled after a real fence or gate.

Climbing and jumping from broad steps, a flight of wooden steps being built for the purpose. Ascending and descending a short flight of circular steps, these steps built for the exercise at slight expense. Climbing up and down a very short ladder. Stepping through the rungs of the ladder as it is laid upon the ground or the floor.

Rhythmic exercises carried out upon a line;
walking slowly or fast, softly and heavily,
on tiptoe, running, skipping, and dancing in
time to music. These exercises may be done
by utilizing the long, straight cracks in a
hardwood floor, the seams in a carpet, by
strewing grain or making a snow line out of
doors.

Exercises in practical life, the most important
of these being brought about by the use of
the dressing frames included in the Montessori didactic materials, and including: buttoning on scarlet flannel, linen, and leather,
lacing on cloth and leather, fastening hooks
and eyes and patent snaps, and tying bow-
knots. Other materials used in these exercises are: brooms and fascinating little scrubbing brushes and white enamel basins with
which the children help to make the schoolroom tidy in the morning. And the children
are taught to open and close doors and gates
softly and gracefully and to greet their
friends politely and with courtesy.

Physical training brought about through play
with a few toys that stimulate healthful mus-

Walking upon a line gives poise and muscular control.

cular exercises and deep breathing. These
toys include rather heavy toy wheelbarrows,
balls, hoops, bean bags, and kites.

Breathing exercises. For these, Dr. Montessori
recommends the march, in which the little
ones sing in time to the rhythmic movement
of their feet, an exercise in which deep
breathing brings about lung strength. She
recommends also the singing circle games of
Froebel. She leads the children to practice
such simple respiratory exercises as, hands
on hips, tongue lying flat in the mouth and
the mouth open, to draw the breath in deeply
with a quick lowering of the shoulders, after
which it is slowly expelled, the shoulders returning slowly to their normal position.

Exercises for practice in enunciation, including
careful phonic pronunciation of the sounds of
the vowels and consonants and the first sylla-
bles of words. This practice in the co-ordination of lips, tongue, and teeth not only helps
the child to clear speech but leads to a
quicker grasp of reading.

Each of these physical exercises has its basis in
child interest. *Your* toddler instinctively pulls

and climbs, stretches, and scrambles about on the floor, longs to dress his own fascinating, wee body, and play into the activities of the home. He loves marked, rhythmic music and longs to hear those jingles and nonsense ditties of childhood's literature in which syllabic sounds are emphasized and repeat themselves.

" Not commands, but freedom; not teaching, but observation," Dr. Montessori begs of mothers. So she has taken these instinctive activities of the little child and, using them as a basis, she has built upon them her system of physical training for the baby, a system that needs no bidding, " Do this," because all children love to climb fences and play with buttons and stretch little limbs on the floor, and keep time to rhythmic music.

Every Thursday morning a crowd of thirty or forty eager tourists from all over the world wait with impatience to be admitted to the Montessori school on the Via Giusti, Rome. Silently, led by a white-robed sister, they enter the schoolroom and seat themselves in quiet expectant rows to watch the miracle of Montessori physical freedom. A hush, a tinkle of child laughter, and the babies flock in from the garden. Noiselessly, gracefully,

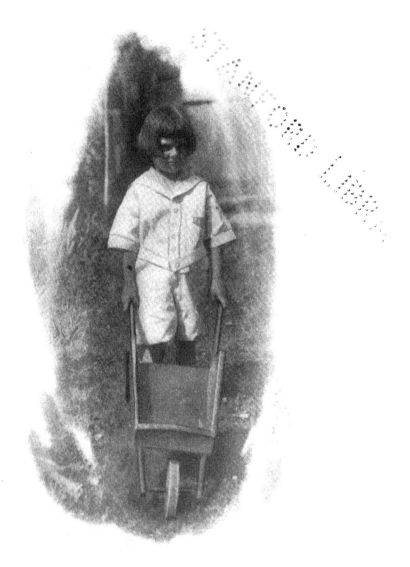

The kind of toy Dr. Montessori recommends for
physical development.

with no rude jostling or crowding—and alone—
they greet each visitor with outstretched hands.
Then, like a bevy of little men and women, eager
to work, eager to achieve, they hasten to the cabinets that hold the didactic materials, to choose
their material for the day. Nothing drops, nothing is broken, no child hurts his neighbor in his
haste, and they find their places, some stretched
out on the floor, some seated at the white tables.
When the hour for the midday meal comes, the
materials are as carefully put back in their places
in the cabinet and the little ones lay the tables
for luncheon. To see a child balance a tray that
holds five filled tumblers, to see another child
bring in a huge bowl of warm soup and serve it
with no mishaps, these interest curious sightseers
as much as the Roman Colosseum or the Roman
baths.

But isn't, after all, the child who has come, by
natural steps, to this control of his mind and body
the normal child? Are not our children, whom we
feed and dress and lead and fasten into high
chairs, the abnormal ones? It is vastly easier to
lace a child's shoes, to hold his hand when he
goes up and down steps, to fetch and carry for

him, than to teach him this muscular co-ordination, but it is just this careful teaching of the
simple things of life that makes the Montessori
child a sight for tourists.

"What makes these children so good?" I heard
a visitor ask her neighbor one morning as she
watched the Via Giusti little ones.

A number of factors contribute to the goodness
of the Montessori child, but one of the most important of these is that he "knows himself." He
knows his body, what it can do and what it must
not do. This physical freedom leads naturally
and surely to freedom of the spirit.

THE FREEING OF OTELLO, THE TERRIBLE

Montessori Awakening of Conscience Through Directed Will

HE was so wee a *bambino* to have absorbed so much brutality in his heart. Not quite three summers and winters old was Otello when his mother pushed him across the threshold of the big, cool, white room of the Trionfale Public School at Rome that houses a Montessori Children's House. There she left him after a volley of guttural speech that told the little dark-eyed girl directress how uncontrolled and passionate was this baby of Rome, a quaint little " man " in stuff dress and bare legs and torn shoes who looked with stolid wonder into the happy eyes of the other babies.

At first it seemed as if the mother were right. In an awed whisper to Dr. Montessori the girl directress spoke of Otello as " the terrible." He met love with apparent hate, kindness with malevolence, sociability with taciturn aloofness. Did little Mario with painstaking effort lay a carpet of beautifully tinted color spools in careful order on his table; then Otello swooped down from his watchful corner and with one sweep of his fat hand wrought confusion in the beauty. Did a stone lie, harmless, in the school garden; Otello found it and used it with dire results. Did Valia, the toddler, with much toil fill her small wheelbarrow with a precious load of sticks ready to trundle it across the playground; Otello intervened, overturned the barrow, and gloated over Valia's tears.

From his first day he showed an amazing inventiveness along lines of disorder. To tear a finished picture that his little girl neighbor had zealously colored, to swoop down upon the heights of the pink tower whose perfect building some other baby had just achieved in a patch of sunlight on the floor and overturn it—these seemed to be Otello's most joyful triumphs. And always, as he planned some act of disorder, he looked up, expectantly, for the blow, the harsh command with which the misdirected force of childhood is so often met by the brute force of the adult.

But these never came. Instead, he saw a group
of sympathetic little ones run softly across the
wide spaces of the room to help Mario in rear-
ranging his color spools. There was no thought
of him, Otello the law breaker, but only the love
of Mario in their hearts.. In place of the reproof
that he almost longed for, that he might meet it
with rebellion, he felt the touch of warm lips on
his forehead, and he heard the soft voice of the
directress:

" Ah, Otello, that was *wrong*."

There was no other word of blame, no command, *you must not*, for him to meet with his
marvelous strength of will and, *I shall*. He might
choose the thing that was wrong—or——

It was one sweet spring morning in Italy that I
saw the miracle happen to Otello, a morning when
the free breezes from the Roman hills brought
heavy odors of grape and orange blooms and the
birds sang their freedom outside the windows of
the Trionfale Children's House. Otello sat in a
little white chair in front of a little white table,
suddenly quiet and thinking. He saw, all about
him, other little white chairs and low white tables.
If he wished he might choose another chair; no

one would insist that he stay in one seat. The
brown linen curtains at the windows rustled pleas-
antly with the perfume-laden wind. If Otello
wished he might go out in the playground for a
breath of that wind. No one would prevent him.
In front of him he saw another large room with
a piano and low white cabinets filled with fascinating Montessori materials, and colored rugs
for spreading on the stone floor, and many babies,
of his own kind, sitting there busily at work. A
child might dash over and spoil the work of a
dozen children at one attack. Or a child might do
a little experimenting himself with these materials
that so engrossed the others. Otello chose the
latter course, and going to one of the cabinets,
he selected one of the solid insets, a long polished
wood frame, into which fit ten fascinatingly smooth
cylinders of varying diameters. Holding the
cylinders by their shining brass knobs, he put them
in their proper places in the frame, took them out,
put them in again a dozen, a score of times. Unconsciously he was training his sense of touch,
but more than this, he was exercising his conscience in a new way. A small cylinder refused to
fit in a large hole in the frame; a large cylinder

could not be forced, no matter how strenuously he hammered it with his little clenched fist, into a small hole. Before Otello put each cylinder in its proper place, he tested it with a larger or smaller hole.

"Wrong!" he whispered to himself in the first instance; and,

"Right!" he ejaculated when the good, smooth little piece of wood dropped out of sight in its own hole.

After almost three-quarters of an hour of this will training, for the little child who persists in a piece of work and completes it is taking the first steps toward properly directed *will*, Otello looked up from his work. Mario, his neighbor, bent over the color spools again. From the pocket of Mario's apron protruded one of the crown jewels of childhood—a big glass marble. Otello had no marble. With all the longing of his heart he had wanted one. Mario bent lower over his color matching and the shining glass sphere, as if it were alive, slipped from his pocket, dropped to the floor, and rolled across to Otello.

With quick stealthiness Otello grasped it in his eager little fingers. It was *his* marble now; no one had seen him take it; in his little brown palm it held and scintillated a hundred colors. How happy it made him to own it; he would slip it into the hole in his shoe to keep it safe until he reached home! But, even as he made a hurried movement to hide his booty, his prisoned soul burst its cocoon. With one of the rare smiles in his eyes that one sees in the undying children of Raphael, Otello ran over to Mario and dropped the marble in his lap.

Otello had taught himself the right and he had made the right his happy choice.

The old way of helping Otello, of helping *your* child to right action and self-education, was to command. Yesterday, we said:

" You must do this because I tell you to; this is right because I say that it is."

Dr. Montessori gives us a new, a better way of educating little children. Before we present her didactic materials to a child, before—even— he leaves his cradle and his mother's arms, we will give the child his birthright of freedom; physical freedom, mental freedom, moral freedom. The place of the mother in education, Dr. Montessori tells us, is that of the " watcher on the mountain top." She observes every action of the child, helps him to see the difference between right and wrong, but she leaves him *free*, that he may train his own will, make his own choice, educate himself.

How can we help our children to the goodness that little Otello has found? What had he missed at home that was supplied to him in the Children's House?

The root that is denied space by its earth mother to stretch and pull and reach does not grow into a tall, straight tree. The bud, shut off from its birthright of sunshine and moisture, does not unfold into perfect flowering. The child who is choked at home by an artificial environment and chained by the commands of his parents will develop into a crooked, blasted man. Dr. Montessori told me that her first word to American mothers is this:—

"Free your children."

Every child is born with an unlimited capacity for good. His impulse is to do the good thing, but we so hedge him about with objects which he must not touch and places which he must not explore and inaccuracies of speech which confuse his understanding, that he rebels. With the force of a giant, the baby uses his will to break *our* will. This is right; he was born as free as air, and we act as his jailers.   Presently, his thwarted will finds other outlets, and we are confronted with a little Otello.

We have thought that to " break " a child's will was the first step toward giving him self-control. We say to a child:

" Don't be capricious! "

" Don't tell lies! "

He is capricious because we have so often interfered with his normal child activities, because they made him dirty, perhaps, or caused a litter that we thought disorderly.   He lies because we have not explained his world to him, or because he fears us.   Seldom is a child capricious or untruthful unless we have made him so.

The Montessori directress at the Trionfale Children's House, first of all, patiently observed Otello. At the end of a week's time she knew more about him than his mother did, for she had recorded his height, weight, chest, and cranial development and had discovered that he needed physical exercise to help his mental development.   We will watch *our* children's bodily growth more carefully than we have in the past if we are to be Montessori mothers.

She never commanded the little fellow whose ears were so deafened with the many commands of his mother that he found it a psychological impossibility to obey. Instead she had faith that his new environment, her careful pointing out of right and wrong, and the ordered activities brought about by the Montessori didactic materials would loose his spirit, which had been like a butterfly stabbed by the pin of a scientist.

So we will be patient with our babies and watch them and wait expectantly for the unfolding of their minds and souls which will surely come if we supply the opportunity.

Dr. Montessori gives us a new word for the home and she blots out an old one.

" Why? " is our new word. We will observe the minutest activity of the home child from its first month to the time when it leaves the home for school, asking ourselves the reason for each activity.

" Don't! " is our blotted-out word. No activity of a child should be inhibited unless it is morally *wrong.*

From babyhood to the age of six years almost

every free movement, every free thought of the child has a meaning in relation to its bodily and mental growth. If we suffocate children's activities, we suffocate their lives. The good child is not the quiet, inactive child. The perfect child is not the child who is nearest like man.

The only way to keep a child still is to teach him orderly movement. The only way to keep him from handling our things is to give him educational things of his own to handle.

It is a more fascinating home occupation than any which you ever attempted, this Montessori way of observing your child. He is your own life flower, a bud, now, but with the power of sure, beautiful unfolding into bloom. Your part is to watch the process of this unfolding, and to surround the child plant with light and nourishment and *freedom* for growth.

You thoughtlessly say, " Don't sit on the floor and play; you will soil your clothes."

" Walk faster and keep up with my footsteps or I will not take you out with me to-morrow."

Dr. Montessori tells us that the limbs of the little child are very short in comparison with his torso and tire quickly from holding up his body

weight.   If his legs are to grow straight and
strong he must follow his own inclination and sit
and lie on the floor when he plays; he must not
be required to keep up with our longer stride in
walking.   We were thoughtless when we commanded *don't*.   Dr. Montessori shows us the *why*.
These actions of the child were wrong only from
our standpoint.   We have to cleanse soiled clothes;
we think that we have no time to walk slowly.
But in the Children's Houses no child is ever required to stay in his small white chair or to keep
his work on his low table.   He is free to work on
the floor in any position which makes him physically comfortable and soft rugs are provided for
this purpose.   No Montessori child is commanded
to stay in line and " keep up " when the piano
gives the signal for a march or one of the gay
Italian dance steps.   Otello and Mario and Piccola, the babies, drop out for a few seconds, seat-
ing themselves for a space of rest, and when their
fat legs are ready for more muscular exertion,
they again join the other children.

But this freedom will make my child fickle, lacking in concentration, you say.

On the contrary, it leads to concentration.   The

Montessori-trained child who has never been prevented from doing a thing unless it was wrong and who has been allowed to carry on any activity which it chooses; free play with outdoor toys, the Montessori physical exercises, sense-training, drawing, suddenly arrives, at five or six years at a most unusual amount of concentration. From a free choice of occupations that lead to the exercise of the muscles and the senses, the minds of these little children order themselves, and the children are able to concentrate on one line of thought for long periods.

In the Children's House of one of the Model Tenements in Rome, I saw a little girl come quietly in at nine o'clock, button on her apron, and seat herself with a book. She read, happily, for three-quarters of an hour, hardly lifting her eyes from the pages, although twenty-five other little ones were carrying on almost as many different occupations all about her. At the end of this time, she closed her book, crossed to the blackboard, looked out of the window a moment, and wrote in a clear hand the following childish idyl to the day:

"The sun shines," it began. "I smell the orange flowers and the sky is blue and I hear birds singing. I am happy because it is a pleasant day."

Do we find such concentration in our children whom we teach according to rule and in masses? We have thought that to educate was to formulate a great many rules and make our little ones follow them, but our new Montessori ideal is a very different matter—that of leaving Life free to develop and to unfold.

The American child has the strongest will, his gift from a vital heredity, of any child in the world. His father and his mother have, also, this splendidly forceful inherited will. Parent and child tilt and bout in a daily fight, and if the parent comes out triumphant and succeeds in breaking the child's will there is a deadly wrong done. That is why our reform schools and prisons are so full of strong wills, beyond bending.

We must let our little ones blaze their own trails, provided, of course, that they are trails which lead in the right direction. We must, also, let them make their own decisions, and if occasionally they prove to have been wrong, the experience will have helped them to decide wisely the next time. We will, also, put into their hands the self-corrective didactic apparatus of Montessori, which has a distinct ethical value in the training of the human will.

Education to be vivid and permanent in the child's life should be worked out along lines of experience. To say to a child, "Don't do that; it isn't right," is to make a very inadequate appeal to one, only, of his senses, that of hearing. To put into the child's hands the blocks of the Montessori tower so carefully graded in dimension that it takes exquisite differentiation to pile them is to give him a chance to learn through experience the difference between right and wrong by means of three senses. He hears a possible direction as to their use, he touches them, he sees the perfectly completed tower. In like manner the broad and long stair, the solid and geometric insets, all contribute their quota to the sum of the child's perfectly directed will control.

The average home is full of mediums for helping a little child to develop along lines of willed control. To concentrate upon a bit of constructive play until it is finished, to learn orderliness in putting away playthings, or to do some simple home duty that will be carried over from day to day, all are important willed activities. To do whatever is in hand, building or drawing or picking up toys, or bathing or caring for a doll or a pet, or helping mother as well as possible, is, also, very vital will-training.

Dr. Montessori helps us to a hopeful outlook on the subject of child will. Our Otellos are not, after all, terrible. The child who is most difficult to manage is, with Montessori training, the child who turns out to be best able to manage himself.

THE CHRIST IN BRUNO

About the New Spiritual Sense

WHEN Bruno was a little fellow, his mother and father were killed in the Messina earthquake.

Because he was one of so many left-behind babies, he was quite neglected, and he grew up to four years as a weed grows. Sometimes one *madre* of the tenement mothered him, sometimes not. At times he was fed, at other times he starved. Because of the great fear that came to him with the blinding smoke and the twisting red river of molten lava and the death cry of his girl mother that day of the earthquake, Bruno's mind seemed a bit dulled. He was often confused by the commands of people who tried to take care of him and so could not obey. Then they would strike him. And he heard very vile language spoken and he saw very evil things done during his babyhood in the tenement.

When Bruno wandered across the threshold of the Via Giusti Children's House in Rome, he seemed like a little alien among the other happy little ones who were so carefully watched over, so gently led. For days he sat in silence, his great, frightened blue eyes watching to help him dodge the blow that he expected but never felt; his lips ready to imitate the vile speech that he had known before, but which he never heard here. His timid fingers fumbled with the big pink and blue letters that the other children used in making long sentences on the floor; they tried to button, to lace, to match colors, but not very effectually. It was as if the great fear of his babyhood had shadowed his whole mental life and left him powerless.

One morning Bruno's dulled blue eyes glimpsed an unusual stir among the children. A new little one had come and, full of disorderly impulses, had snatched at the varicolored carpet of carefully arranged color spools Piccola had placed on her table, scattering them to the floor. Red, green, orange, yellow, Piccola's painstaking work of an hour lay in a great, colored, mixed-up heap. Piccola's eyes, still pools that reflected all the hazel tints of fall woods, grew blurred with tears. She dropped her curly head in her arms and sobbed, big, gulping sobs that wouldn't stop, that strangled her. Bruno, watching her, found his muscles. He ran to her, putting one kind little arm around her waist, and with the other drew her head down to the shoulder of his little ragged blue blouse and smoothed her hair, talking sweet, liquid non-sense all the time that made Piccola's sobs grow less and less, and comforted her. When she smiled and drew away to watch the group of children who had hurried to pick up her colors for her, Bruno slipped back to his corner and the old, dull look settled back in his face.

"The little man has the conscience sense. He shall have a chance to use it," thought the Mon-tessori directress who had been watching the scene.

And because she wanted his soul to grow strong, even if his timid fingers couldn't, she often stopped by Bruno's chair to hold his hand, kindly, for a minute in hers, or just bent over him, smiling straight down into his face.

"No one will hurt this little man of ours. He loves us and we love him," she assured Bruno over and over, until one day her patience reaped the prize of Bruno's answering smile and she felt his two hungry little arms clasping her.

She strengthened his beginning friendship with

Piccola, the color-loving, reckless, daring little maid, whom all the children loved to love and loved to fight. When Piccola brought an unusual treat in her luncheon basket, a leaf-wrapped packet of dried grapes or two luscious figs instead of one, the directress suggested that she share with Bruno, who had no one to tuck a surprise in his basket. As the two child faces drew close above the feast and the little hands fluttered together over this friendly breaking of bread, Bruno's eyes sparkled. He was reading his first lines in the primer of love; he was finding his sight. And in return Bruno helped Piccola to rake leaves in the garden, he unrolled and carefully spread upon the floor the rug upon which Piccola wished to curl herself and sort letters; he hastened to add his strength to hers when the drawer that held the letters stuck; he fought Piccola's street battles for her.

Soon Bruno's loving busy-ness so increased that he found things to do almost every second of his happy days in the Children's House. No longer the little cowering, cringing, inactive child of a few weeks past, he was an alert little man whom I instantly watched, because his activity was so unusual. When the line of children, two by two

and clasping hands, in their pretty custom of wel-
coming visitors to the Via Giusti Children's House,
tumbled in each morning, Bruno always headed
the line. He held by the hand the smallest, new-
est, or the most timid child, dragging it in his
eagerness to teach it to shake hands and say
good-day. He would "hold up" the line because
he had so much to say in his welcome to the
strangers who had come to spend the morning with
the little ones.

"See our Signorina; is she not *kind?*

"This is our room; do you like it?

"There is Margherita; she *writes!*

"This is Piccola, who reads!"

In breathless sentences, Bruno's heart interest
worded itself. Then, as the others settled themselves for the day's work, Bruno began his day
of service. He was the Loving One, the Helping
One, the Comforting One of the Via Giusti Children's House. Was any child left without a glass
of water at the luncheon hour, Bruno fetched it.
Did the little girl waitress for the day forget to
fill a soup plate from her tureen, Bruno re-
minded her. If the three-year-old started home
with his cloak unbuttoned, Bruno, feeling in his

tender little heart the chill wind of the Roman hills, buttoned the cloak for the baby. If a toddler tumbled down, Bruno picked it up and examined it for bumps, and started it safely on its way again. He fetched and carried, watched for chances to help, to champion the weak, to wipe away anybody's tears with the hem of his apron.

The seat he most often chose was under a cast of the Madonna. Sometimes he sat quiet for long spaces, looking at it. "Bruno calls the Madonna his *madre*," whispered Piccola one day.

"Who is that big, homely child?" asked a visitor, pointing to Bruno putting fresh water in a bowl of roses that stood under the cast. "Isn't he older than the other children?"

"Older—yes, in spirit," answered the far-seeing directress. "He is our little Christ-child."

So he is *our* little Christ-child. Wherever there is a child in a home, Dr. Montessori tells us, there Christ is. She discovers for us a new sense, the "conscience sense," only waiting for an opportunity to exercise itself and, in the exercising, unfold and bloom and ripen into the fruits of the spirit. If being an orphan and hungry and beaten

and knowing vile things couldn't hurt the soul of
Bruno, think of the possibility of Christ in *your*
baby.

Children grow, mentally, through the right exercise of the senses. To see and to be able to dis-
tinguish between beautiful colors and beautiful
forms; to discriminate between sounds that are dis-
cordant and sounds that are harmonious; to know
rough things and smooth things, round things and
square things, velvet things and linen things, by
touching them with the finger tips, this we know
is a starting point on the road of the three R's
of everyday education. Dr. Montessori guides us
a lap farther in the new education. She sees, born
with every child, eyes of the spirit and slender,
groping fingers of the soul that look and reach
for the good. To help a child to use his spirit
eyes and his soul fingers means to give him a chance
to exercise his conscience. It is a new sort of
sense-training that means his finding the three
R's of the life of the spirit: faith, hope, and
charity.

How shall we help a child to exercise and train
his *conscience sense?*

Dr. Montessori tells us that if we but watch a

little child's free, spontaneous use of his soul fingers, his daily loves and hopes and faith, these will shine for us as a Bethlehem star-path leading us to the manger-throne of a King-in-the-making. As we are turning a child's tendency to *handle* into mind-training, we will turn his manifestations of inner sensibility into morality.

It is quite ineffectual to say to a child:

"You must love your neighbor."

Of course he will try to do the thing that we ask of him because he is a very kind little person, ready to put up with the inconsistencies of his elders and willing to try to obey; but it will be a makeshift sort of love, not free and a flowering of the child's own heart, but built upon what we tell him about love. This makes of children little puppets.

Dr. Montessori says: "Watch *how* children love and *what* they love."

You know *how* your child loves—with the thoughtless abandon of pure passion. That he interferes with your important occupation, crumples your immaculateness, has a soiled face and sticky fingers when he kisses you, do not enter into his thoughts. That anything should interfere with his caresses would wound his heart. If you were disfigured or maimed, he would still vision you as the beautiful mother whom baby eyes see only with the eyes of adoration.

Is this a love that we can teach?

You know *what* your child loves. There was the ugly yellow puppy with muddy feet that stained your new rug; don't you remember how the Little Chap sobbed so long, and then woke up in the night crying, the day you sent away the yellow puppy? He loved, too, the dirty rag doll that you burned and the broken toy that you threw away, and that little street gamin of a newsboy who stands at the corner in all kinds of weather. He doesn't love ceremony and money and the opinions of other people as we do. The Little Chap goes out into the highways and byways for his stuff of love. And he doesn't care if the thing he loves is ugly, or old, or halt, or lame, because he sees, with his soul eyes, behind the veil of appearances to the *real of it*.

Your child is born with faith and hope, too. If you tell him that the moon is made of green cheese and that a stork dropped him down the chimney, he believes you, and when he grows up and catches you in the lies, he has one less peg in his moral inner room to pin his faith in the divine to. If you tell him that you will take him to the circus, and then let your bridge party interfere with that promise, the Little Chap is going to be less hopeful that God will keep His promises, for you stand for the divine in the Little Chap's beginnings of spirituality.

Dr. Montessori says that we often crush the child's conscience sense by not giving him an opportunity to exercise it as he is led to, instinctively. We must let our children, in their baby days, love *as* they wish and *what* they wish. We must be quite careful to give them true conceptions of the strange world in which they find themselves, and we must make only good promises to children and use much vigilance in keeping those promises.

Dr. Montessori sets another guidepost for us in the star-path by which our children will travel across the desert of unbelief to the manger where God, incarnate, lies. She tells us that, as the Ten Commandments were a very simple set of laws for the Israelites, and John, in his preaching of simplicity, paved the way for Christ, so the first religious teaching of the little child should have this same quality of directness.

The child's first religious training will consist in a discrimination between good and evil.

"It was good of you to share your sweets with sister. When you ate your chocolate, alone, yesterday, I was sorry, because it was selfish."

"It was thoughtful of you to fetch grandfather's cane for him. Some little boys would not have been so kind."

"You must not scream and kick when you are angry. It is wrong!"

We might say in contrast; we do, ordinarily, say:

"You must share because I wish you to."

"You must be kind because the world likes gentlemen."

"You mustn't scream and kick, because you give me a headache and mar my furniture."

Such commands are quite ineffectual, because they call the child's attention to us and not to his own acts. But patiently and effectually to see that the Little Chap knows the difference between good and evil and practices good instead of evil—this gives him a chance to train and

strengthen his conscience sense and forms the beginnings of his moral life.

" But how shall I give my child an idea of God? "
thousands of thinking parents object.

It isn't necessary to give the idea of God to
your child.   Dr. Montessori tells us that *every
child has it.*

We think that we must do so much teaching in
order to educate the little child's mind, or his
soul.   In fact we need to do less teaching than
watching, less pruning than watering.   After observing our little ones' spontaneous manifestations
of love and giving these a chance to increase, and
meeting them with encouragement after conscien-
tiously pointing out to them the good and the evil
of life and insisting that they choose the good
and reject the evil—we discover a miracle.   God
comes to the little ones.

Bruno, starved in his mind and starved in his
heart, and never having heard of things of the
spirit except in terms of the vilest blasphemy,
found God as naturally as he would find the first
gold blossom of the broom braving winter's frosts
on the Appian Way.

Our own Helen Keller, deaf and dumb and blind,

knew God before anything that her teacher could tell her about Him had pierced the dark wall of her sleeping senses.

Dr. Montessori asks us to prepare the way for this miracle in our homes.   She says that she would like to suggest to mothers a new beatitude, " Blessed are those who *feel;* " and we add,

For they find God.

MARIO'S FINGER EYES

Montessori Sense-Training

YOUR little one, Mario, might have been, big eyes instantly glancing a bit of color, something that moved, something that could be handled or broken. All his four years he had been fighting his mother, his home, the world—a one-sided fight, too, for everybody and everything always triumphed over him in the end. He was so little and so ineffectual to do battle.

And the times when he had been punished for breaking his mother's cherished plates with the pattern of raised roses—plump and red—for clutching in loving, chubby, grimy hands the soft silk window curtains or the bright velvet table-cover could not be counted. Yet Mario was cheerful and uncowed and continued the struggle, the impulse for which had been born with him, to use his fingers in learning about the world of *things*.

To check this impulse was the object of everyone who had anything to do with little Mario. There was his grandmother in a wonderful silk headdress and a yellow wool shawl, fringed; she would not let Mario clutch the cap and then feel of the shawl, as his fingers itched to. There was the old fruit man at the corner near Mario's house; he shook a stick at children who handled his round and square measures, his fruits, and vegetables of so many different shapes. There was always his *madre*, who pursued Mario from waking to sleeping time, interfering with his activities.

"Mario, don't run your fingers along the window ledge; don't handle the door latch. You will soil them. You must not play with copper bowls and pots; they are for cooking, not for little boys."

As the warfare continued, Mario grew bolder. To be stopped when one is playing with a fruit measure or a door latch or a bright, red copper bowl with no malicious designs upon these but only to satisfy a sense of hunger for knowledge of form, hurt his spirit.

"I *will*," he announced one day, when his grandmother tried to rescue her cap from his deft fingering, and he pulled off one of the long, silken streamers.

"I will *not*," he further asserted when his mother wished the copper pot to cook her beans, and when she tried to take it from him forcibly, Mario stamped and shrieked and struck his *madre*.

The habit of saying "I will" or "I won't" in situations that demand the will to decide, "I won't" or "I will" is an easy habit for a little child to form and a most dangerous one, morally. It is seldom a self-formed but a parent-stimulated habit. When his mother put Mario, for reformation and "to get rid of him," in The House of the Children at the Trionfale School in Rome, it was with the assurance:

"He's a bad little boy. He never does what he ought to; he's always in mischief."

"What should be a little child's 'oughts' the first years of life? Isn't what we call getting into mischief, perhaps, the big business of childhood?" we asked ourselves as we watched Mario in his Montessori development. So, at least, Mario's teacher decided.

"Go as you please, do as you wish, play with whatever you like—only be careful not to hurt the work or the body of any other little one," were the words that turned Mario's struggles to educate himself into a joy instead of a fight.

Sitting in the light of the Roman sunshine and the smiles of the other children of the Children's House, Mario began to do the thing he was born for in babyhood—he began to *see with his fingers*.

I watched him for days, such a blessedly good, chubby, curly-headed little man that my arms ached to hold him, instead of leaving him free to trot from one occupation to another, busy, concentrated, educating himself. Mario's mother, his wise old grandmother, the canny fruit seller,— none of them had known how blurred the world looks to the eyes of a little child. Many mothers are not able to see with the eyes of a child. We grown-ups who comprehend a beautiful landscape, a lovely fresco, a piece of miracle machinery, a fragile porcelain vase, a statue, an immortal pile of architecture instantaneously, analyzing the form that makes the beauty, never stop to think how we grasp it, mentally. It is the color and curve of the landscape, the combination of lines in the fresco, the " feel " and contour of the statue, the " fit " of the machinery, the design of

Replacing the solid insets by the sense of touch
alone.

Building the tower and the broad stair.

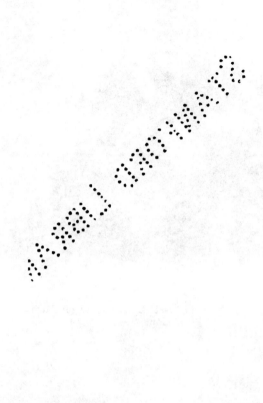

the vase, the combination of geometric figures in the building, that make the beauty. The artist, the inventor, the sculptor, the architect, saturated their finger tips, then their eyes, and last their brains with a knowledge of line and form before they saw Fame reaching out her hands to touch theirs. Every little child is born with a longing to *feel* line and form, not perhaps for Fame's, but for Knowledge's sake, and we crush the longing when we say " don't touch."

Intent, engrossed Mario worked for days until he grew expert in piling, one upon the other, the graded, rose-colored blocks of the Montessori Tower. Soon he could erect the tower, blindfolded. Just a fascinating play it looked, as interesting as is the play of our babies with their nested picture blocks, but it was play with a purpose. It taught Mario to *feel* and then to discriminate, mentally, between objects that differ in dimension, one from another.

Then came the fun of laying in order the graded blocks of the Montessori Broad Stair. Building steps, it was, as all home children instinctively struggle to build steps with their blocks, with dominoes, with pebbles and rocks of different sizes.

Why do children like to build steps; is it not because they live in a world of *high* and *low*, and *higher* and *lower* things? We grown-ups say, " It is a beautiful sky-line, the tall and low buildings rubbing shoulders," or " The clouds are banked in a red and gold mass." How did we learn the beauty of gradation of form in a city, in nature? Once when we were as little as Mario we tried to build stairs, we jumped, happily, from one step to another; we climbed, we learned height and depth by *feeling* them. So, Mario learned to see minute variations in the height of objects through the broad stair.

He spent hours fitting the little wooden cylinders in their places in their frames. How he had longed to play with the vases and jugs at home, some tall and some short, some thick and some thin. And how many times his mother had prevented his digging rows of little holes in the garden in which to fit, first, a fat thumb, then a slim forefinger; last, a tiny finger! With the Montessori geometric insets, he could enjoy this hole play, and, at the same time, learn, through *feeling*, to recognize very fine differences in height and breadth. One day Mario found a little set of drawers in the big white material cupboard at the Montessori School. It made him remember his grandmother's great shelf of drawers with the polished brass knobs. In these were hidden fascinating, musty-smelling wool shawls, silk scarfs, soft embroideries, and stiff, bright ribbons. Mario's secret happiness had been to climb upon a stool, clutch a brass knob, pull, and then delve pink fingers into the sense-feeding horde of stuffs. He would close his eyes and enjoy the *feel* of them, but there was always the rude awakening.

"Naughty Mario—don't touch." But now he had these other drawers full of stuffs to open, to empty, to sort the contents, to crumple the stuffs in his hands, and then match velvet to velvet, silk to silk, wool to wool, blindfolded. It hadn't been shawls and scarfs and embroideries and ribbons that the little man wanted, but a chance to use his fingers in learning to recognize the qualities of objects; rough, soft, smooth, stiff.

Otello brought a great, crimson poppy to the Children's House one day. Poppies to the Roman baby are as dandelions to our children, so lavish a gift of the nature mother as to be of little value after the first bloom colors the grass. Otello's impulse was to pull off the already dropping petals of the flower, but Mario rescued it from the ruthless baby fingers. Holding the fragile stem between forefinger and chubby thumb, he ran the other forefinger lightly over the surface of the velvet-soft petals of the poppy. Then he ran to baby Valia and touched her leaf-soft cheek with the finger that taught him how like a flower petal in softness is the flesh of a child.

It was so daily an application of newly-gained knowledge as to be unnoticed save by a wondering onlooker. It was the mind enrichment through sense-training denied Mario by his home and offered him by Montessori.

The frames for geometric insets enthralled Mario next. To take out of its place, fit in again, and refit a dozen, twenty times the different sizes of flat wooden circles, squares, triangles, rectangles, and other forms kept the little fingers busy and the opening mind concentrated for long spaces. The wooden insets are large, shining with polish, and easy to handle because of the brass knob attached to each. As Mario lifted one out of its place in the form board, he ran his fingers around the edge, then around the empty place in

A fineness of perception is developed by discriminating
different textiles blindfolded.

touch intelligently. The lure of the senses is a spiritual spell in childhood. If we catch it, then, and turn it into channels of knowledge, we may develop a Marconi, conqueror of space; a Rodin, conqueror of form; a Burbank, conqueror of life— a Carrel, conqueror of death. At least we will have developed an observer who knows how to use his senses in the practical living of life.

the board. Soon he could do this with closed eyes, fitting wooden figures of many different shapes and sizes correctly in the form board. He matched these forms to corresponding paper forms mounted on cards and then to outlined forms.

Here was a circle like the top of the red copper bowl, and a smaller circle like the top of the yellow majolica mug that held his milk in the morning. Here was a rectangle like the kitchen window at home and a triangle like the glittering one the band man struck to make music. Kitchen utensils and home furnishings and the street band are as vastly interesting to all children as they were to little Mario, interesting because they are things of color and texture and shape and sound.

One morning Mario showed his teacher one of the rectangular geometric insets. "The window in the church," he explained. Then he picked up a rectangular inset. "This is like the flower-bed in the Gardens," he announced.

Your child struggles to educate himself through his senses as did Mario. You, too, perhaps, not seeing the inspiration in the active little fingers, say, "He gets into mischief all the time." It is

distant wheat field—these fed his soul and satisfied his hunger.

Because the State was blind and thought that
to fight is more vital than to paint beautiful
pictures, the grandfather of Raffaelo was forced
into the Italian army.   The day that they substituted a gun for his crook and threw away his
palette, they killed his soul.   The grandfather of
Raffaelo made a very poor soldier, indeed.
The little boy that he left at home on the Campagna grew up, and was a poor soldier, too;
and when he had finished military service
he married and went to live in a tenement in
Rome, and in due time little Raffaelo was
born.

It was all quite commonplace, and like the story
of many other families.   But it had, too, its element of the unusual.   With those long-ago, shep-
herding days on the Roman Campagna, a gnawing
hunger had begun.   It wasn't a body hunger,
but a hunger of the spirit.   It killed the body
of the grandfather of Raffaelo—spirit hunger
is more destructive than a hunger for bread.
Down through the years it took its gnawing way.
It killed the youth in the father of Raffaelo and

it took possession of him in the gray streets of
the city and stifled his manhood.

Then the hunger pierced the spirit of little
Raffaelo, and that was where it stopped—a cruel,
unsatiated thing. With the gathered strength of
all those years, it starved the baby.

He couldn't have explained in words just what
he was hungry for. In fact he couldn't explain
anything very well, being not quite three years
old. Only, he was continually unsatisfied when
he looked at the ugliness of the dull walls of his
home, and when his mother took him along the
hard, gray streets of the city he tugged and pulled
at her hand whenever he passed a corner flower
stand, or a cart piled high with a mass of colored
vegetables.

Raffaelo was beauty hungry, as his father had
been and his grandfather. And no one knew it;
and no one would have cared if they had known.

No one?

Little Raffaelo trudged across the court one
morning to the Children's House in the Scuola
Famagosta, near which he lived, and there found
a kind welcome and a happy, busy community of
children like himself. Neat, in his clean apron,

and with big, questioning eyes, he sat apart from
the others in one corner of the room, watching.
Certain of the children were writing big, plain
script on the blackboard; others sat quietly reading to themselves from big picture books. Raffaelo's glance shifted from these to a child who
stood near him, working at a low table. What
had he brought from the white shelves in that big
wooden box? Raffaelo wondered. Why was he
turning the box over? But the table was suddenly
covered with a mass of color, such as only the
Romans know how to dye. From the box came
reel upon reel of ravishingly colored silks, every
color that tints sky and field and garden—crimson, orange, lemon, the deep green of the grass,
and the gray green of the olive leaf; the blue that
makes wild iris and children's eyes, the purple
of grapes when the sun shines on the vineyards.
If Raffaelo could have counted, he would have
known that there were sixty-four of these flat,
white wooden spools, wound with eight colors and
eight of each color, showing almost all the grading of color that makes this old earth of ours
so lovely.

The colors trickled like a life-giving stream into

To match the colors two by two is the first exercise

Raffaelo's starved senses. He reached for the color spools, snatching a great fistful away from the other child.

"*Mio; mio!* Me; me!" he cried.

They *were* his. Some of us steal bread when we are hungry. Some of us steal love when we are famished for it. Children steal because we or the world have starved them of something which they crave for their natural, best development of body, mind, or soul. The habitual public school teacher, the average mother of to-day, would have said:

"Give those colors back. It's wicked to take something that is not yours!"

The directress of this Montessori school, in which teaching and mothering are practiced in new ways, watched Raffaelo for a moment, asking herself:

"Why does this child steal? Is he blind to law because his need is so great?"

Then she crossed to Raffaelo, bringing with her a handful of color spools—two red, two blue, two yellow.

"These are yours," she said. "Will you give your little neighbor's colors back to him, because it was not right to take them?　When you have carried to him every one of the spools, return to me and I will tell you about *your* colors."

Happily, Raffaelo did as he was told, receiving his first lesson in ethics before he had his first color lesson.　Returning, he stood, wide-eyed and fascinated, beside the directress as she held out to him two of the color spools.

" This is *red*," she explained, laying the red spool on the white table in front of him, and waiting a moment or two, that he might make the mental association between the name of the color and the color itself.　Then she showed him a blue wound spool.

" This is *blue*," she said, laying his spool at the opposite side of the table from the red one, and again waiting for Raffaelo to make the association of name and color.　Taking the next step in this Montessori teaching, she pointed to the red wound spool, and asked:

" What is this, Raffaelo? "

" Red," he laughed back.

" And this? " pointing to the other one.

" Blue! " Raffaelo almost shouted in his delight at acquiring knowledge.

Then came the last step in Raffaelo's lesson.
Holding out the remaining tablets in the palm of
her hand, the directress said:

"Show me red, Raffaelo. And show me blue."

With no mistake, the little color lover selected
the red, the blue, and placed each on his table,
matching them to the corresponding spools.

"These are yellow," the directress explained
to him, giving him the two remaining spools. Then
she left him, having given him the food for clear,
colorful thought for which two generations of
thwarted painters had made him long.

All the morning Raffaelo played with his six
color spools, gathering them together into a pile,
handling them, holding them up to the light, that
he might watch the play of sunshine and shade
upon their beauty, pairing them upon his table,
repeating to himself: " Red, blue, yellow!" Sometimes he watched his small neighbor, who had
grown very expert in color lore and could name
all the colors and lay the spools in chromatic
order on his table, eight rows headed, severally,
by black, red, orange, yellow, green, blue, violet,
and brown, and each row containing eight gradations of its color.

When this child completed his series of orderly color scales he went to the window and looked out at the Roman hill rising back of the school. To the child who had not received Montessori color teaching, the hill would have been a shapeless, colorless bit of earth. To this child, who could see color in its finest gradation, it was a landscape where one could trace the gold outline of orange and lemon, the red tiling of a vine-tender's house near the top and back of it a sky that was violet— not blue. He looked at the hill for a long time. Then he selected an outlined picture of a tree, and looking intently at a box of colored pencils, selected one that was just the color of a cedar and proceeded to fill in the outline.

To Raffaelo, the child was a spellworker. Watching this fascination, the directress gave Raffaelo a box of color spools, emptying them out and allowing him to try and differentiate the colors, putting each back in its right compartment in the box. She did not burden his mind with names. He was feeding his senses by just handling and feeling the colors, and he was unspeakably happy. When the noon hour came, he did not want to go home. When his bedtime came,

Grading each standard color and its related
colors in chromatic order.

All the colors of nature may be found.

that night, he escaped from his mother and ran
to the window, looking out. The night before, he
had looked down at the soiled, unbeautiful street;
to-night he looked up. The sun was just setting,
a ruby ball in a sea of amber.

" See!" Raffaelo shouted, pointing to the sunset. " Red; yellow!"

As his mother picked him up and carried him
away from the window, he looked deep down into
her eyes. " Blue," he said, seeing them for the
first time in all their beauty. The hunger of Raffaelo was fed.

Every child is color hungry. Your child may
be a painter in the making, heir to a century-old
talent that somebody had to bury, but which would
not die and rose and haunted. Or he may be an
average child who will be happier and better all
his life if he can see each fine gradation of color
that tints the sunset and can feed his soul on a
beautiful Titian or a Fra Angelico.

We have thought that we were teaching our
children color when we called their attention to
a colored object. A child is much more apt to
associate taste with the apple which we show him
when we try to give him a color lesson, and quite

possibly we make a false statement when we say
that the apple is red. Very few apples are *red;*
they are dark red, light red, orange, or yellow
in tint. Why not begin the other way round, as
Dr. Montessori does, and teach pure *color,* giving
the child the joy that comes from discovering for
himself just what pigment nature used in painting the apple.

In teaching children color, we will use, if possible, Dr. Montessori's own box of sixty-four color
spools that include almost all the tints and shades
of the prismatic colors, black to gray, and the
scale of browns. If we are not so fortunate as to
be able to use this apparatus, which is a most
careful and scientific analysis of color, we can try
to study color ourselves, and point it out to children as it is found in the home in textiles, silk
and worsted, papers, flowers, and colored crayons
and paints.

In teaching color at home we may all follow
Dr. Montessori's own simple method. The Montessori directress might have tried to teach Raffaelo color as we, in America, teach our children,
saying:

" See the ball; it is red. The forget-me-not is

blue.   See the pretty robin redbreast," and in making these statements confusing in the child's mind the concepts of toy, flowers, birds, and colors when all he needs is *color*.   Every child wants to make his own application of knowledge.   Instead, the girl who had been trained under Dr. Montessori had followed the only true method of teaching any fact, the method that lies at the basis of Montessori education miracles.   Dr. Montessori says that teaching must be *simple* and *objective*. There hasn't been enough of " calling a spade a *spade* " in our American schools and homes.

Show your child red, or the letter A, or a moral fact—it doesn't matter much which—and name it *red*, or *A*, or *right*.

Ask him to tell *you* just what you told him about it.

Ask him to pick out red from other colors, or A from other letters, or a moral act from immoral acts.   This is Montessori teaching reduced to A B C, but it is teaching that is successful.

Our homes may be made as full of color and beauty for little children as are the Children's Houses.   The use of the prism, the Montessori color spools, the color top, our beautifully graded colored crayons and water colors for filling in outlined pictures, a study of the colored papers to be had for paper dolls' clothes, the daily watching of the color changes in sunrise and sunset—all these open the spirit eyes of the child. Then we will lead children to notice and appreciate harmonious blending of tints and shades in our walls, our rugs, our gardens, our picture galleries.

Of what value is it that the child's chromatic sense be trained by learning to know and discriminate between red, blue, and yellow, and from this to acquire a facility in knowing the scale of grays and browns? It means more for the child than just the soul-satisfaction that comes from learning how to use the eyes. It means *starting* the brain machine and then looking out for the switch.

The first morning that I met little Mario, one of my child Montessori friends in Rome, he looked me over from head to foot, ran to a color box, selected a color spool of the exact shade of gray blue of my suit and showed it to me joyfully. In almost the same second that he made this mental decision, he saw that the quick movements of little Valia were threatening the safety of a glass vase that stood, holding flowers, on a table at the opposite end of the room. Like a flash, Mario ran, held the vase, and prevented the catastrophe.

To be able to think down the color scale from blue to a blue that is mixed with gray; to be able to think in another kind of mental scale from cause to effect—these are both *chromatic* mind operations.

To know color means satisfying your child's beauty hunger. It means, also, starting him on the road to logical thinking.

THE GOING AWAY OF ANTONIO

Directing the Child Will

Antonio had a longing to *do*.

Since babyhood, he had watched the *madre doing* about the house, the *padre* who left each morning and returned each night after a day of *doing* somewhere.

All of Antonio's most interesting world of little things revolved about a circle of persistent activity. The earth in the garden moved with its life of roots and bulbs, the very small ant creatures crept about from sunrise to sunset with their sand burdens, the gray branches of the olive opened to show their hidden treasures of leaves; the birds built; Luigi, the old farmer beyond the garden, continually loaded and unloaded his creaking yellow cart. Antonio absorbed this life energy with as much hunger as he ate his soup and figs.

"I will, also, *do* all day," he decided, ready to try the adventure.

"I will make a little garden," he chose one morning.

The spade was too huge for baby fingers, the frost-hardened ground demanded force in digging. Some hyacinth stalks, just pushing their odorous, purple way up through the mold, were broken by Antonio's eager effort. Still, the little boy persisted, endeavoring to accomplish the task that his imagination pictured—a little round flower-bed of his own, made by his hands, and in which flowers of all colors might raise their heads overnight. Now he smelled them; now he could feel their velvet-soft petals.

"Stop! Come here, naughty Antonio. You cannot make a garden; you are too small. And you dirty your clean apron."

Antonio dropped the spade as the words of his *madre* shrilled through the air. He sat down in a discouraged heap on the edge of the path. Always, his *madre* could persist in tasks, but he was continually interfered with. Why?

But with the buoyancy of childhood, the little man suddenly jumped up. A rattle of tin bells and a strident shriek of protesting, ungreased wheels were the prelude to Luigi's approach. In his cart of oranges and lemons, with bunches of poppy and wheat stuck in the chinks, Luigi rode down the lane. His smiling face was as russet and wrinkled as an old nut, bits of miracle-hiding clod stuck to his blue smock. As he passed, he tossed an orange to Antonio.

"I will be a farmer. How fine to earn money for my family, as Luigi does," little Antonio decided. He ran to the house and, pulling out his little cart, loaded it with some of the vegetables that stood in baskets in the kitchen. He trundled it up and down, calling his wares as he had heard Luigi. At first his *madre* laughed. Then, watching him, her smile furrowed itself into a frown.

"Why play that you are Luigi, who is only a farmer?" she expostulated. "Be a great general. Here are your toy soldiers." She pulled his little cart away from Antonio and pushed into his arms a box of gaudy tin soldiers.

"Drill them; command them," the *madre* urged Antonio.

Antonio watched, sadly, the demolition of the little cart which stood for playing into bread-winning. His soldiers were painted manikins, not very steady on their legs and only slightly interesting. He tried to stand them in rows and they all tumbled down. He changed them for his ball, and his *madre* suggested that a picture book would be a better plaything for the house, taking the ball away from him. When he was absorbed in the book, she tore him from it for a walk with her in the streets.

So it always happened with Antonio. No one allowed him to *persist* in an occupation, no one allowed him to *choose* what he should do, and each day's activities were *decided* for him.

From a strong-willed baby whose impulses were all good, Antonio drifted into weak-willed little boyhood. It was as if he were daily followed by a spirit of indecision.

"Shall I concentrate on this play?" Antonio would ask himself, and in reply the spirit which had risen from his babyhood influences whispered in his ear, "No."

Then came his manhood, and he asked himself the same question.

"Why persist? It is easier to shift, continually, from one occupation to another, not doing anything long, or well.

"Why trouble to choose? My mother made

decisions for me when I was a little boy; the public
school teachers chose my studies for me; now that
I am a man, let other men think for me. I have
no power to control my will."

How simple a solution of the life question! The
fingers of Antonio that had itched in babyhood
to make the earth bloom and to earn bread closed
quiescently about a dagger handed him by a man
who said, "Come with me; do as I decide for you."
The crime Antonio did was not his fault, nor the
fault of his accomplice. It was the fault of his
madre.

Dr. Montessori tells the story of the child whose
will is misdirected in babyhood. He is the child
whom his mother and the public school system
mold into a lump of putty by thinking for him.

The greatest problem of to-day in child-training is, how shall we help our little ones to strength
of will? Civilization is being sapped by our weak-
lings. Home-training, the public schools do not
develop character. Dr. Montessori tells us that
this is because parents and teachers do not know
what will, fundamentally, is.

Dr. Montessori says, "To will is to be *able*.
The little child who persistently struggles to pile

block upon block until a miniature tower or castle rises under his fingers, *persisting until he completes* the labor, is taking his first step toward will-training.

" Family life, trade life are built up on this persistency. Whether it shows itself in loving, or giving or working, constancy makes the social will. Every motor activity is an act of will, and constancy in *right* activities makes character."

Other great teachers have said the study of mathematics and the dead languages, the military discipline of the army, mortification of the flesh, make character. To train a child's will we feel we must crucify it upon the cross of our desires. A child must obey us, we say, follow our caprices and chisel himself into a likeness to us, because we wish him to be like us. Why should children be little men and women? Are we so sure of our own perfection that we have a right to force our personality upon that of our children?

Dr. Montessori gives us a new rule for developing character in children. She says:

" *Seek the child's first longings* if you would train his will. Give him the foundation of will by helping him to concentrate on something he instinctively craves to be busy about and so lay the foundation stones of his character."

The little child's first impulses to be active are good. He wants to be about his father's business by taking part in the activities of the home. We make our children weak-willed by our own capriciousness in interfering with their attempts to be active. We dress them, we feed them, we wait on them, we drive them to play, we lead them; we put them in kindergartens where they flit from one occupation to another without an opportunity to concentrate on one; we put them in schools where their days are cut up into little bundles of study, tied with the iron chains of Schedule that make prisoners of children; we continually decide for our little ones and kill their characters with the sword of misdirected kindness.

Some children are born with the color of painters in their souls, and we punish them for soiling *our* pictures and mussing *our* tapestries and trampling upon *our* gardens. May we not look beyond their impotent acts to the spirit-longing that prompted them and put into their hands the best in the way of color: paints, crayons, books, flowers that will satisfy their desires and give them an opportunity to concentrate on the activity they instinctively crave. So they gain will power.

Other children are born with a vision of the builder in their eyes, and we thwart them when they try to use the furnishings of the home in a process of reconstruction. May we not equip our little architects with materials for building, call their attention to the classic in architecture and art, give them a chance to build their own characters?

Most children are born little cosmopolites—small world citizens who explore with the greatest interest the strange, new environment in which they find themselves. These are the children whom our present system of coercion in home and school hurts most. We crush their wills by not giving them an opportunity to follow their instinctive interests in babyhood. The innate impulses of such children are good. They must explore and produce around themselves. They must be helped to wise choice and right decisions. So they grow to willed man and womanhood.

Is this following of personal impulse, as shown in Montessori-trained children, productive of better concentration than we find in our public schools to-day?

Part of the Montessori didactic material for teaching numbers consists of a cardboard case into which cards bearing big black figures may be slipped, giving the child an opportunity to work out number combinations. A little lad of five discovered one morning, when I was observing at the Via Giusti Montessori school in Rome, that he could slip into his case cards in regular succession that would count to one hundred by fives. He spread out his cards upon the sunny floor, provided himself with the polished counting sticks for verifying each operation; then kneeling in front of his counting frame, he went to work, alone, concentrated.

It was visiting day at the School. Tourists, teachers, students lined the room to the number of forty or fifty, leaving the children scant space to work, and as the little boy's numerical adventure began, they crowded closer to watch him. An American public school child would have grown restive and self-conscious, but this little Montessori lad might have been alone in the Sahara, so quiet, so unheeding of anything but his own occupation was he. The number cards are large, and it took a good many to reach one hundred. The little fellow spread them out in the center of the floor, then carried the row under the chairs of the visitors, not seeming to notice the presence of the grown-ups.

The morning grew gold with noon, and the other children, quietly putting away their materials, spread the low tables for the midday meal. Little white bowls, snowy napkins, carefully laid spoons —then the steaming chicken broth. Still the little counter did not move. He had reached seventy-five, after verifying every number he had registered in the case. One of the wee waitresses for the day carried his red and green luncheon basket and set it down on the floor in front of him; he did not heed it.

"Why doesn't somebody stop that child's counting and *make* him eat his lunch," expostulated a nervous American school teacher, watching. "Children should be made to do certain things at certain times," she explained.

Just then the boy slowly and with great pains fitted a figure one and two ciphers into the counting case. Like a little conqueror he stood up, folded his arms, and looked at the perfect result of two hours' willed, concentrated work. A smile broke the baby face into dimples, and running out into the garden, he began to play like a little colt. He was not tired. He was not hungry. He was only joyful at this conquest of his will.

Montessori will-training proves itself in results.

The practical life and gymnastic exercises of the method have a peculiar value in relation to the strengthening of the child will. Once a child has learned to inhibit his scattering muscular disorder in such co-ordinations as are involved in dressing and undressing, feeding himself, bathing, taking part in the everyday work of the home as far as possible; in walking, running, marching, skipping, dancing to music, and the other rhythmic and gymnastic exercises involved in the Montessori system, he has fixed a permanent habit of muscular control which establishes, also, mental control. To be able to place dishes and silver in an orderly way on a table, to carry and balance a tray containing several filled cups or glasses, to be responsible for a certain drawer or cupboard shelf or case in which are contained play materials is to be able to control mind as well as body.

The muscular education of Montessori that has a direct bearing upon the direction and development of the child's will is included in the primary activities of everyday life, in walking, greeting, rising, and handling objects gracefully; in the proper care of the person, in taking part in the management of the household, in gardening, in such handwork as clay modeling and drawing and in all properly co-ordinated gymnastic and rhythmic movements. This new and direct will-training is possible in any home.

A more subtle but quite as important phase of control of the will through *doing* is seen in connection with the child's use of the didactic apparatus, especially the solid and geometric insets, the tower, and the broad and long stair. In the use of each of these there lies for the child a very important quality of self-correction. A broad cylinder will not fit into a narrow hole; the plain rectangular inset cannot be made to slip into the outline of the board intended for a square; a misplaced block or rod spoils the sequence of form and number in the tower or the stairs. After being shown the perfect way of carrying on each of these exercises, the child experiments with them alone. He discovers that the material admits of two possibilities: error and success. The success possibility is the greater, however; it is easier to drop a solid inset into an opening that fits than to endeavor to crush it into a hole that is too small. So, by persistent and repeated experiment, the child attains a habit of correcting his own mistakes. This habit he carries over into the other willed activities of his life.

The Montessori method presents three steps in the home development of the child's will. First, we must give our children as wide and free an opportunity as possible to be active, especially with their hands, along those lines which will lead to muscular control. Second, we must not interfere with a little child's concentrated occupation through play. Last, whatever task we set for him to do, we must outline a right way in which it should be accomplished and encourage him to correct his own errors in it.

A mother said to me recently, " I keep the children in bibs still, although I suppose they have outgrown them. We can't have our meals delayed while we wait for three active youngsters to fold napkins."

Dr. Montessori would have patiently and pains-takingly instituted the napkin habit, realizing that in even so simple and homely an operation as fold-ing a square of linen neatly lie undreamed possi-bilities of strengthening a child's will.

ANDREA'S LILY

The Nature-Training of the Method

" IF you put it to sleep in the good brown earth, Andrea, if you tend it and wait with patience," explained the Signorina, " you will see a wonder."

Andrea turned the brown lump over and over in his hand. He rubbed it on the sleeve of his apron. He held it up to the light. It had no appearance of wonder; it was cold, it did not shine, it would not reflect the light. Did the Signorina, after all, *know*, Andrea wondered, as his big, wistful eyes looked out from the warm cheerfulness of the schoolroom to the chill, windswept spaces of the Convent garden. Memories of great banks of gold daisies, roses so heavy with crimson petals that they bent as low as the little green winding paths, winds sweet with perfume of the grape filled Andrea's imagination. These had made the garden of the Children's House yesterday. But how different it was to-day!

108

Could the dead bulb which was his, now, to tend, to watch, to believe in, make for itself life and bloom?

Andrea, the matter-of-fact little man of four, was skeptical.

"Of what use is it to plant?" he queried.

"Try it! I will help you dig a hole," Bruno, the helpful, volunteered.

"We will not let any child take it out of its bed; we will protect it for you, Andrea," assured Piccola, flashing eyes full of the fire of anticipated battle.

"Cover it carefully with earth, and only be patient," reiterated the Signorina. "Believe me. It will make for you a surprise."

It was a momentous morning that marked Andrea's planting. His fat fingers, holding the trowel, trembled. Like a circle of small acolytes, Bruno, Little Brother, Piccola, and the rest, white aprons fluttering in the wind, watched the sacrifice. Covered out of vision in its winter grave, the bulb disappeared and the children, now almost as skeptical as Andrea of its possible germ of life, ran back to their work in the schoolroom. All, save Andrea.

His baby hands, like two warm, brown leaves, fluttered over the earth prison of his bulb. Kneeling down on the frosty path, he bent low, listening, as if he hoped that he might perhaps hear the groping of new roots. It was all very cold, and perfectly still about the place where he had buried his little dead hope, but Andrea whispered to it:

"I will wait," he promised.

The bleak Roman winter spent its chill days. Flurries of snow shrouded the garden and the wide doors of the Convent, open so many days of the year, were closed. Andrea did not forget his bulb, though. Every day he ran out to the place where he had buried it, eagerly watching for the slim green fingers he had been told would push their way through the frosty earth. As the weeks drifted by, and while the garden was still bare, a strange thing happened to the soul of little Andrea. The patience that was necessary for keeping alive his hope in the brown bulb began to show itself in other ways.

"Andrea no longer frowns when the little brother of Bruno takes away his letters," the Signorina exclaimed. "Instead, he goes to the

cabinet and fetches a buttoning frame, offering it to the little one instead of the letters for which he is not ready."

In other ways Andrea proved his patience. A bit of drawing that he had finished, hastily, a month before and with crooked lines, now held him concentrated for an hour, and was completed with exquisite neatness and exact contour of line. At the midday meal of the children Andrea did not, as formerly, beg to be served first, nor did he open his little green basket of luncheon before the other children. It was as if the slow-growing bulb which was working its sure way up through the bare ground to the sun had its counterpart in the unfolding root of patience it had planted in the heart of a little child.

After a little, the winter melted into a spring of yellow lilies and long sunny noons and laughter at all the gray street corners. Andrea came earlier than the other little ones to the Children's House each morning, that he might spend a half hour with his little green watering pot in the garden. He met Bruno and Piccola with an air of assurance that set him apart from them. He held his head very high in those days because of realized hope which he had made his own.

"Andrea is our little gardener," the children said to each other, watching his triumph.

Then came a visitor's morning at the Children's House of the Via Giusti Convent. The children's greatest happiness was to welcome these grown-up friends who came to learn of the little ones the truths of life. Among the throng of students, tourists, curiosity seekers, earnest thinkers, a woman whom the children knew entered and slipped into a waiting chair. She had been during the winter a frequent visitor, quiet, sympathetic, with deep, smiling eyes. Then she had not come to the Children's House for many days.

But they remembered her still. As flowers turn to meet the sun, they twined about her, feeling her soft, strong hands, touching with eager finger tips the dull, clinging garment that draped her. Ah, they drew back, consulting together in little questioning groups.

"She wears now a black dress."

"Her eyes are full of sorrow," they said.

"The Signorina tells us that, now, she has no *madre*."

Andrea, apart from the others, listened, sympathetic, wondering. Sorrow should be replaced by happiness, of this he was quite sure. Was not the most unhappy child in the Children's House the one most loved, most helped by his Signorina? Had he anything to offer this friend that would give her joy? He ran to her, grasped her hand in his; dragged her from her chair, across the threshold, into a luring little green path dented with many child footprints.

"See!" he exclaimed. "I waited."

Where Andrea had laid away his hope, a tall, straight stalk of heavily odorous lily bloom pointed skyward. The earth that it had scattered in its bulb-bursting still surrounded the strong, green stalk. It was a chalice of the spring, a symbol of life that is eternal.

"I planted it and I waited," Andrea repeated. "All the children waited with me.

"It blooms," he finished, laughing up into the joyful eyes that smiled back, comforted, into his.

Life is a phenomenon in which no force is wasted and out of whose apparent death there continually confronts us the wonder of new life. Some of us are blind to the lessons Nature teaches, but little children may be led to *feel* nature facts that spell for them faith and hope and sympathy for all time.

Dr. Montessori tells us the place of nature in education. We will put the planting and tending of little gardens, which are the child's own, above the place which such work has held, formerly, as a part of manual education. We will make gardening a means of leading our little ones to *observe* the phenomena of life, to be *patient* in waiting for that life to manifest itself, and to be very sure in the hope that fruition will come.

Does *your* little Andrea, your child who has come to you with such a divine curiosity about life and so quick a sense to feel it, have a chance to be, himself, a part of the miracle by helping something to grow? To plant a seed, to surround it with all the best conditions for growth, to tend it, to wait for its flowering—this is Montessori development possible for any child.

Many of us feel that we are bringing our little ones into a nearness with nature when we show them beautiful pictures of flowers, lead them to exquisite gardens in which they must not pick the flowers, or take them to walk in our parks. This

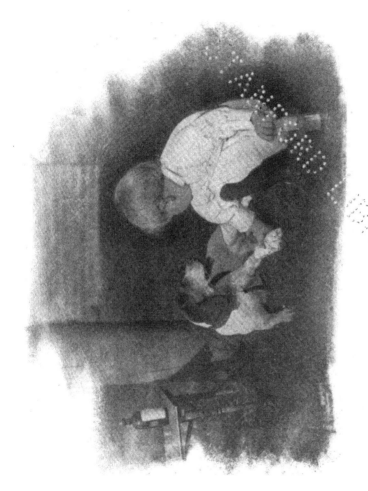

The loving care of a dumb animal results in child sympathy.

is not making nature a force in the life of a child
as Dr. Montessori would have us. Children must
touch and *feel* and *act* to know. The flower that
is too beautiful for little fingers to gracefully pick
and give to a friend as an offering of love should
have no place in our gardens. The grass that is
too soft to bear the prints of little feet is not
the right kind of grass for an American park.

To plant a bean in a clay pot that stands on
a city window sill; to tend the plant that grows
from the seed, saying with surety, " Some day
there will be beans on this plant," means more to
a child than to be told the life story of an orchid.
It is the difference between *thinking* and *feeling*.

A rake, a shovel, a little basket, a cart, a watering pot—these are all Montessori didactic materials that any child in any home may have. A
flower pot in a window, a window box, a tiny plot
of earth in which to plant, one of these is possible
for each of our children, and the flowers and fruits
that result from the nurture of child hands mean,
for the child, flowers and fruits of the spirit.

The world of every day is full of gardens for
our children to plant, and helpless, dumb animals
to be fed and cared for by child hands. It has

been so easy for us to do these things ourselves that we have not stopped to think what it means in the life of a child to have *helped something to live*.

There is the bare seed, without shape or body or hint of promise. There is the green, groping plant that appears. Then comes the sure blooming that rewards child patience. Some plants are more slow to sprout than others; there is the fruit tree that did not sprout in the child's life but whose pink blooms he now sees. So it may be that the good hope planted in his own heart while he is still a little fellow may not fructify for a long time, but he will wait, with patience and faith.

Caring for plants and dumb animals has further life application for children. We continually serve our little ones. Because we love them, we do too much for children; we take from their eager hands all works of service for others which would do much to develop the latent sympathy that buds in every child's heart, only waiting for the slightest stimulus which will make it expand and develop.

Your child needs one plant that is dependent for life upon his care. He needs one pet that

To feel that something is dependent upon him for care and food helps a child to reverence life.

demands his daily forethought and vigilance to safeguard its life. As he waters the plant, watching it and providing for it the best conditions of light and freedom; as he feeds his pet, your child feels and is able to image the watchfulness of his father and mother who feed and care for him, who gave *him* life. He will form a habit of *feeling* and *helping*, and will grow up loving, sympathetic, and with a reverence for the phenomena of life.

There are also the rewards that nature gives children, coming as marvelous surprises, unexplainable mysteries, beyond the work of hands. The little ones at the Via Giusti Children's House in Rome may be often seen clustered about a blossom that has unfolded while they were at home and waits to greet them in the morning—so different, so vastly more beautiful than the tiny seed which they sowed. These children would not care for a crude toy, given them as a reward for their labors. The toy can be explained; it is made of wood, or iron; it has no connection with the child's work for which it is given as a prize.

But here is a lily, the reward of their work, but unexplainable; the product of a force that is miracle working. Its petals are like wax. With their sensitized little fingers the children touch them; no, they are not wax. No one can tell of what texture these petals are made. The flower has its own perfume, haunting, individual. Andrea did not plant those petals, he did not smell that perfume when he buried his hope. It found its own body.

So with the greatest simplicity, Dr. Montessori brings to children the truths learned from the cultivation of *life*.

THE MIRACLE OF OLGA

Reading and Writing as Natural for Your Child as Speech

" I HAVE something strange in my pocket," Olga exclaimed to the group of little ones who clustered about her, twittering, poised in excitement like a flock of baby birds.

It was just after the luncheon hour in the Children's House, and the babies filled the sunshiny paths of the garden or loitered in happy groups in the cool stone cloister of the Convent.

" My mother told me the story of Pinocchio, the wooden marionette, who had so many adventures with a cricket for his friend, and also a fairy with blue hair. It is too wonderful a story to have been born in the mind of my mother. She *found* it. I have it now, with me! "

There was a breathless hush among the little ones. Pairs of blue and hazel eyes fixed every motion of the little brown maid in the bright pink apron. With slow dignity and an effect of great mystery Olga thrust one chubby hand into the depths of her pocket. The fingers fumbled a bit, then pulled out a crumpled, printed page torn from a book. Dropping, cross-legged, to the stone floor of the cloister, Olga unfolded and spread out the page in her lap. The others bent over her with all the curiosity and reverence that would be stimulated by a conjurer.

"Here is the mystery," Olga announced, indicating the printed words. "I have discovered that *this* is the hiding place of Pinocchio. I have torn it out of the book that I may carry it, always, in my pocket."

"Olga will carry Pinocchio in her pocket," the others exclaimed in hushed whispers, scattering to talk over the matter. "Is it possible that we, too, could find Pinocchio, as Olga has, and carry him in *our* pockets?"

So it happened that the mothers of the children of the Via Giusti School began to miss pages from their newspapers, their magazines, their books.

"We have very bad, destructive children," they decided, not stopping to question the reason for their little ones' sudden interest in written language.

So it happened, also, that the directress of the school, always alert to watch the mind phenomena of her children, noticed that many children in the school had torn bits of printed pages hidden in their apron pockets, in the soles of their shoes, in their caps. In the midst of their most fascinating work, they would stop, take out these scraps of print, smooth them, and trace the letters with baby fingers.

"We have stories with us all the time; Pinocchio is ours," they said.

"My little discoverers!" the far-seeing directress exclaimed. "They are not wilfully destructive. They are ready, now, to create a new language that will carry them farther than spoken words can. Their longings shall be satisfied."

One morning the directress gave Olga new materials with which to work. There was a big, white wood box divided into twenty-six compartments, and in each compartment there was a huge letter of the alphabet cut from pink or blue cardboard. The blue letters were consonants; the pink letters were vowels. Seated on a soft green rug on the floor, Olga spent hours taking the letters out of their places, piling them in a colored heap of many fascinating curves and angles, then sorting them and putting each back in a compartment in the box.

Sometimes, as Olga worked, the slim girl directress dropped down on the rug beside her. Picking up one of the cardboard letters, she would say:

" This is A, Olga."

" This is A," Olga would repeat.

" Can you show me another A? " the directress would then ask. And Olga would, readily, pick out a similar letter.

" Where is A, Olga? " was the last question in this teaching as Olga selected from the twenty-six letters another A. So the little maid of four years soon knew all the letters by name and sound. And presently she was combining them to make words and short sentences.

As she laid together the letters that made up each word, the words that combined to make sentences, the directress analyzed each word for her, phonetically. Soon, by hearing a word, distinctly pronounced, Olga could select from her box of

Building words with the movable alphabet.

pink and blue symbols which represented sounds to her now those letters which were necessary to spell the word.

The directress presented to her smooth white cards, on which were mounted large black letters cut from coarse black emery cloth, as rough as sandpaper. These letter cards Olga held in one hand, tracing the outline of the letters with the fingers of her other hand and saturating her senses with the *feeling* of the letter shapes. Soon, she could name any letter, her eyes closed, by the sense of touch.

At the same time that Olga was learning to *see* and *feel* letters, she was being helped to the muscular control involved in writing. Upon a sheet of white paper she laid one of the Montessori geometric insets, a square, and selecting a brightly colored pencil, she drew the outline of the square upon the paper. Then, with the slanting lines used in writing, Olga filled in the outline of the square. At first, the lines were crooked, extending beyond the boundary lines of the square; but as she repeated the exercise, filling in with color other forms, outlined triangles, rectangles, circles, leaves, flowers, trees, and figures of children and animals, her muscles strengthened and she could control her pencil with the utmost precision.

Two months after her first interest in a printed page had shown itself, through no training save these sensory and muscle exercises, Olga made the miracle of graphic art her own. She went to the blackboard and wrote in clear, flowing script: " I read, I write."

Your baby tears picture books and magazines; he leaves great, unbeautiful scrawls upon wall paper, woodwork, and sidewalk. He upsets the ink and breaks the pens in his father's study. He wishes to handle all the books upon the library shelves. We punish him for these acts because we think them wanton. Dr. Montessori tells us that these child activities indicate an instinctive interest in the *symbols* of that new art, human speech, which he is making his own in the first years of his life. They tell us that we have made a mistake in not giving children an opportunity to teach themselves to read and write at the same time that they are mastering spoken language. The two interests present themselves simultaneously in our little ones. Children who tear books and scribble upon walls and interfere with the im-

maculate order of our home secretaries are not
little mischief makers. Like Olga, and the other
babies in the Children's House, they are trying to
make their own the story that you read them.
Even the tools of writing for little children are
gilded with the same air of mystery that touches
the untranslatable black print.

The wonder teaching of Montessori, by means
of which, after two or three months of preliminary
exercises, little ones " explode " into reading and
writing, may begin at home. Any watchful mother
may lay the foundations for this educational
marvel.

Have you watched the process by means of
which the little Stranger who came to you from
the unknown masters the strange speech of the
home in which he found himself?

Are you helping or hindering him in his struggles to make language his own?

The beginnings of speech in the baby consist
in repetition of syllabic sounds which he hears in
his home environment. His vocal cords and tongue
educate themselves through pronouncing articulate sounds. First come the labials. Then the
little one combines consonants and sounds, saying:

" Ma-Ma. Pa-Pa." The mechanism by means of which the sense of hearing combines with the vocal cords in helping the two-year-old to speak makes it possible for a child to learn several foreign languages in the first five years of his life.

The child is making his own dictionary in babyhood and at a phenomenal rate of speed.

Dr. Montessori says that we may help a child to beautifully phonetic speech and a large vocabulary if we will eliminate all baby talk from our nurseries, and see that the little one hears only good models of speech. Clear-cut, carefully pronounced words, well-planned and euphonious sentences, rhythmic poems and classic stories read to our children, these will train the sense of hearing and lead to a large vocabulary and beautiful pronunciation. Suppose you were learning a foreign language, wouldn't it discourage you to have your interpreter mispronounce, *baby talk* French or German or Italian to you? Our babies find themselves in a land more strange to them than any foreign country we have ever visited. We are their interpreters; let us not put stumbling blocks in their road to language.

Then, sometimes at three years, four, or five

Filling in outlines with color to gain the muscular control necessary for writing.

Learning the form of letters by the sense of touch.

comes the tearing and scribbling stage. Every mother knows it, but Dr. Montessori helps us to a new recognition of its meaning. It isn't a development of the old Adam in your child. It's a guide signal for every mother. It tells you that the intricate human mechanism that makes up the child spirit is ready to learn written language naturally, without undue nerve strain, if only the right stimulus be offered.

It is because we have waited until the instinctive interest in spoken language grows dull and because we have depended upon only one sense, the sense of vision, that teaching a child to read and write has not been the natural, quick process nature means it to be.

If the nursery equipment includes the movable alphabet and the sandpaper letters of the Montessori didactic materials, your little one, instead of tearing letters, may *feel* them, his sense of touch carrying to his mind a telegraphic message of letter form that is registered permanently on his brain. After handling these large, stiff, pink and blue letters for a month or two, after tracing with his sensitized finger tips the rough black letters mounted on the smooth white cards, they are so indelible a part of his mental life that they *must* burst forth into writing without previous training. Don't you remember how your baby by fingering his raised letters on his alphabet-bordered bread-and-milk bowl, by feeling of the raised letters on his alphabet blocks, by building words with the cut-out wooden letters of his letter game, learned without effort on your part how to print? So, by touching the beautiful script letters of Montessori, a child teaches himself to write.

But there is another process involved in the Montessori method of helping very little children to an early mastery of reading and writing. In the public schools a pencil is put into the child's untrained fingers and we expect him to use it in writing with no preliminary help in handling it. We couldn't use a needle in fine embroidery if we had not learned, first, how to thread it. We are not able to paint a picture of a landscape until we learn how to use a brush in outlining perspective. So we make a mistake when we expect that to hold a pencil means to be able to write. We must help children to the muscular control of this tool of writing first. Dr. Montessori tells us that drawing precedes writing.

The Montessori didactic materials for developing in children the muscular control necessary for writing include small wooden tables; flat metal forms cut in various shapes, squares, rectangles, circles, and triangles; plenty of white drawing paper, and good colored pencils of the standard colors and brown and black. Laying a form on a piece of paper, the children draw its outline. Removing the form, they *fill in* the outline, using long, vertical, parallel lines of any color they like, keeping within the contour of the outline. So the child educates his muscles for writing without *actually writing*.

The little ones at Rome soon experiment with combining these forms to make colored borders and flat designs, which they fill in with their colored pencils in very harmonious color combinations. Later, they fill in outlined pictures, using the same free, regular pencil strokes.

The Montessori method of starting reading and writing saves time in most instances. Whether or not, however, it is at four years or five years or five and one-half that the " explosion " into written expression of thought occurs, the process by means of which it is brought about is sure to give the child a firm perceptive basis for reading and writing.

Our ordinary method of teaching reading and writing is a utilization of the sense of sight, alone. In some instances the children in the primary grades of our schools begin writing by a system of tracing letters and words offered them in large script.   This is purely a muscular process and rarely absolutely successful, because it involves fine muscular co-ordination for which the child of five or even six years is not ready.

The Montessori sandpaper letters and movable alphabet offer the child a chance to utilize his sense of touch in learning the symbols of thought. Formerly we showed him a word or a letter as a means for gaining so vivid a mental image of that letter that he would be able to recognize it and write it.   The method of Montessori sends a telegraphic message by two wires to the child mind, a visual and a tactile impression.   The tactile message is peculiarly valuable in strengthening the mental image of the word or letter because of the fact that the child is in a strong sensory motor stage of his mental development. To *touch* gives him stronger mental images than to *see*. To *feel* gives him, also, an impulse to imitate and to express. This is why, after touching and naming and differentiating and recognizing blindfold and building words and sentences with letters, the Montessori child spontaneously writes.

Because we are so anxious for immediate educational results with our little ones, the spontaneous reading and writing of the Montessori method has seemed to parents one of its most important developments. If, in our home Montessori experiments, children do not read and write very early, we are disappointed. We wonder if the system has the value we attached to it. We must change this state of mind.

There is the toddler of three who evinces an instinctive longing to read and write. He experiments with pencil and paper; he shows an interest in the home books, newspapers, and periodicals; he asks what the signs in the street cars and on the billboards say. There is also the child, no less promising, but more interested in objects than in symbols, who does not show these manifestations until the age of five and five and a half years.

We must recognize these signs according to the child's age and take advantage of them. The part of the mother is to watch for the dawning of the interest in reading and writing and to give the child an opportunity to perfect the physical and mental mechanism for it.

Our homes and the educational helps to be bought for children now furnish accessory material for the Montessori process of teaching the graphic art.

The first tracing of the sandpaper letters should be preceded by exercises whose object will be the refining of the tactile sense; dipping the fingers into cold, hot, cool, and lukewarm water; differentiating blindfolded rough, smooth, hard, soft substances; recognizing with the finger tips alone many different materials, paper, iron, wood, velvet, cotton, silk, linen, satin, lace, needlework, and possible combinations of these textiles. These exercises form a most fascinating game for the child, and, through them, he brings to the exercise of tracing the sandpaper letters an exquisitely sensitized touch which results in a clear impression of their form.

As the child uses the movable alphabet upon his play table or builds words and sentences upon a bright rug spread out on the nursery floor, all the activities of the home in which he has a part and all his play life may be used as the basis of his first reading. His favorite toys may be placed about him as he constructs their names and little word stories about them. Large colored pictures of simple design may be laid on the floor as the child combines letters to spell the objects contained in them. The mother may write in large script simple instructions which the child may read and follow:

" Run to me."

" Bring me your ball."

" Close the door."

Innumerable helps are to be procured for the drawing by means of which Montessori establishes the muscular control preliminary to writing. Our art stores and kindergarten supply shops offer beautifully colored crayons and drawing paper at nominal cost. Blocks, the tin utensils of the kitchen, and box covers offer geometric surfaces about which the child may draw, if the drawing board and forms of Montessori are not included in the home equipment. These outlines the child will delight in filling with color, using the diagonal strokes that form a direct preparation for the muscular control involved in writing. Following this coloring of geometric forms is the filling in, similarly, of simple outlined pictures. We find such outlined pictures in large variety in the school and kindergarten supply shops. The toy dealers supply books of really beautiful designs and pictures for coloring. It is also possible to procure sets of cardboard figures, animals, paper dolls, and soldiers which the home child may draw around and color.

One day, after having made his own, through the sense of touch, the form of letters, and after having learned muscular control in *drawing form,* your child will write. How can he help it? You will have established artificial conditions, muscle and sense, similar to the conditions through which he learns to talk.

The baby *hears* speech, and because heredity perfected his vocal cords for reacting upon mental stimulus of the sound—he *talks.* In the Montessori method, he *feels* letters, and through the perfecting of the muscles involved in reproducing those letters which he has made his own by feeling —he writes.

CLARA—LITTLE MOTHER

The Social Development of the Montessori Child

CLARA always saw me before I caught the outline of her cherubic chubby person. She had constituted herself the little four-year-old hostess of the Trionfale Children's House. Her limpid brown eyes shone with welcome to a friend or stranger. Her lips were overflowing with sweetly liquid words of greeting. Her fat arms reached out, her fat legs were winged with her friendliness.

She was the motherly, hen type of child, never so full of joy as when she was greeting someone or organizing a game or taking care of a child younger than herself. An intensely feminine little person was Clara, who would grow up into a kindly, gracious woman, forceful in her own tactful, woman way if she were surrounded by the right influences in childhood or——

I very curiously watched the social development of the chubby little girl in the bright pink frock.

Little Roman babies have the most fascinating play fancies, I believe, of any in the world. Given a cart and a faded flower or so, and Otello was transformed in a second's space into a busy flower vender calling his posies up and down the school yard, offering imaginary bunches and twining imaginary wreaths. A pile of stones left by the architects in a corner of the playground; Mario was suddenly fired with the building zeal of his Roman ancestors. Gathering a group of boys to help him carry and lift the stones, he would construct small models of the immortal walls of the Cæsars and a possible arch of Titus.

Clara played, too, but not so much with *things*, as with *groups*. Her play had the social quality so important in the all-round development of the individual.

She would gather together a group of little ones for a festival procession or a folk dance, apportioning strong partners for the weaker ones and older ones for the babies. She played house daily, but in a different, lavish kind of way. She had, always, eight or ten make-believe children; found room in her house of sticks and stones ·for the fruit seller, the cheese man, the porter, and a stray musician or two. Her strongest instinct seemed to be a collective one. She wanted to brood. She wanted to be, also, a leader.

The Montessori directress let Clara very much alone, smiling upon and encouraging her play, but not trying to mold her instincts. If Clara industriously swept out her domicile with a stick, the directress did not run to her, offering her a toy broom. When Clara was a little slow about going into the schoolroom when the out-of-door period was ended, the directress did not fret at the little maid. She realized that Clara had merged her own personality in the personalities of the group of children with whom she had been playing. She had been so busy preparing her imaginary family for going to school that she did not heed the call herself.

How would the social instinct so prominent in Clara and in several other of the children find vent inside the four walls of the Children's House, I wondered? Would the Montessori system, which has for its basic principle auto-education, this system of perfecting the individual through self-direction, give Clara and the others a chance to develop group activities?

For some time the cool, white schoolroom was the scene of individual work and personal endeavor. Otello worked alone with the solid insets; Mario's fascinated fingers sorted colors. Clara sat on the floor in the sunshine and constructed the tower, but her keen eyes followed almost every movement of the other children. Then, for the school was in its inception and the children were new, came a transition period, when the peace was broken by perfectly normal, healthy brawls. Someone overturned Otello's cylinders and Otello kicked the offender. Several children wanted the same box of color spools at the same time. The directress kindly interfered and gave the colors to Clara, who had been first upon the scene. Clara motioned the crowd to follow her. Now had come her chance. She organized her group. She selected a red spool and spread out upon a white table its beautiful gradations from deepest crimson to palest rose pink. Then she offered the blue spools to Mario, showing him how to grade the varying shades. It was fascinating, Mario thought, to have Clara for his little teacher. He motioned to several of the other children to join them. Tables were drawn up; brown and golden heads bent close together as the little ones dabbled in the colors, advising, helping, learning from each other.

The directress hovered outside of the group, suggesting but not forcing herself upon the children. They turned to her when they needed her, but their greatest interest lay in the joy and power of working and learning together.

As one watched the phenomenon of this natural unfolding of the social instinct in the method, there were daily examples of its spontaneity. The children, from a collection of units, had been transformed into a small community in which there were groups of workers, some large, some small, but all co-operative. The children carried on the sense exercises and took bold adventures into the fields of reading and writing together. The Montessori directress was always their captain and guide, but the grouping and working with some other child or children was the result of childish initiative.

It developed in this way.

The children learned to *live* together. They found that the integrity of Clara's group, of Mario's, or Otello's, was preserved only if the individuals in it gave themselves up to the good of the whole. It was pleasanter to move tables and chairs softly, to wait one's turn, and to avoid jostling one's neighbor. So kindness and neighborliness and gentleness were learned by the children through their own endeavor.

The children *learned* together. There were groups of various grades of age and mental ability. Here the children of three and four emptied out an entire box of color spools and, each choosing a color, helped each other grade. There, a trio of energetic babies slopped in their basins, endeavoring to wash each other to a common cleanliness. In a quiet corner an older child taught less advanced children to spell with the movable alphabet or to work out arithmetic calculations with the rods. This group learning was carefully watched and safeguarded by the directress, but she never forced her personality upon the children. The children, left to their own efforts, found a stimulus to a wholesome kind of competition. They tried to outstrip each other in learning, and put forth more effort than if they had been urged by the teacher.

And, best of all, the children were *good* together.

If one child did anything that interfered with

the rights of the others he was kindly but effectually isolated.   He was denied nothing save his
privilege of being an active, happy member of the
child republic.   To be allowed to go back to it was
his ultimate joy.

The Montessori House of the Children is a place
of more unusual development of group activities
among little children than we have realized.   There
is a larger opportunity for making children into
little citizens than in almost any other scheme of
education.

We have thought that the present practice of
the kindergarten, in which group activities are
organized and directed by the kindergartner, gives
little children the opportunity for the development of the social instinct which they so much
need.   At a signal, they rise and carry chairs,
or march in step, or play a game, but the signal
was given by the teacher.   She directs the game.
We have wandered so far from the leading of the
gentle Froebel whose guiding star was the natural
impulses of individual children in his garden of
little ones.

It is vastly more difficult to lead a number of
children safely through a first transition period,

when all their self-activity turns into channels of disorder, than to check that disorder by force of adult will. This is the task Dr. Montessori sets for us, however, and she shows us, as the result of our patient leading of the children into habits of self-directed order, her peaceful, industrious Houses of the Children. Like a hive of bees, the little ones swarm in the flowering of their interests. They are intent upon community welfare.

The problem of helping a child to be a perfect social unit is as pressing a problem for the home as for the school. We are following the letter and not the spirit of Montessori when we offer a home child the intellectual stimulus of her didactic apparatus and deny him companionship in the use of it. It is eye-opening for a child to so learn form that he can detect slight variation of outline and is able to perceive the beautiful combination of lines which make a cathedral or an arch. It is soul-opening for this same child to help another child to a perception of this beauty.

The three periods of the spontaneous developing of the Montessori children into collective activity, as I observed them, have an even more direct bearing upon the home. Left alone, offered the scientific apparatus for mental, moral, and physical growth, the Montessori children make these important social adjustments.

They learn to *live* together.

They *learn* together.

They are *good* together.

A great deal is involved in the development of each of these adjustments. We must study the method of Montessori by means of which success in group activity is made spontaneous.

To say to a child, " You must be polite. You mustn't be rude. It is ugly to be clumsy. It isn't nice to be selfish," was the part of the older decalogue in child-training. To teach a child by careful physical and rhythmic exercise and through simple acts of home helpfulness, so that he is naturally graceful and courteeous, is the Montessori way. To provide him with play or educational materials which have greater possibilities of interest if shared—blocks, games, handicraft materials—accomplishes unselfishness. Such community play as is found in imitating the activities of the childhood of the race—digging, cooking, collecting, all kinds of building, trade plays, weaving, gardening in groups, and camping—is valuable because it helps children to merge their personalities in the interests and life of a *group*. The center of these child activities is child interest, not adult pressure.

Dr. Montessori makes it possible for little children to learn together, not according to schedule, but in line with child interest.

A mother wrote me at great length and anxiously in regard to what seemed to her a little son's lack of adaptability to the home use of the Montessori didactic apparatus. The boy had toys, books, colored pencils, blocks; he was endowed with a vital interest in the world about him and an alert mind, but he refused to play alone. He preferred playing in the street with a group of other children, their only play material being pebbles, sand, or bricks, to playing at home with his own beautiful equipment.

" How can I persuade Harold to work alone with the Montessori apparatus? " his mother queried.

It was important for this child and for all children not to work alone. Any child will make greater educational strides if the stimulus of other child minds helps his intellectual growth.

To set a group of children of different heredity, different mental and emotional development, and different interests the same task is not only futile but dangerous. It is apt to mold their plastic minds to one line of thinking, is bound to make them slaves of authority instead of free personalities. But to offer a group of children the tools of knowledge as exemplified in the Montessori didactic materials and give them the opportunity to gather in selected, interested groups for competitive research and for helping where help is needed is the most fruitful kind of learning.

This may be brought about in any home where a few children from three to four or five years of age meet regularly under the same conditions for intellectual development that exist in the Children's Houses. Older children may be formed into a neighborhood home study club. Released from the bondage of the iron curriculum, they may find in this club an opportunity for original research along those intellectual lines which interest them most; nature, the practical application of mathematics in measuring and constructing toys, further study of history and literature through story-telling, making and dressing dolls to illustrate historical characters, and the writing and dramatizing of simple plays.

As a further development of the Montessori group activities we see, in imagination, in every community a municipal Children's House. Here, children of all classes, ages, and degrees of intellectual growth might meet, freely selecting from a large variety of materials for mental and constructive development those which they most need. Also, we see them selecting their own social plane, finding help and inspiration in collective work with other children. In this municipal Children's House we would find groups of child artisans, fashioning boards and molding bricks to make the buildings for a toy village. There would be little sculptors and painters, and perhaps a child poet or dramatist. We would see small *modistes* and milliners learning, through designing doll costumes, the finger deftness and artistic sense which come from combining beautiful colors and textiles. Such a Children's House would have its own kitchen, where the children could study foodstuffs and cook and serve simple meals. Music would be a development of the group activities. This would constitute a laboratory for the most fruitful kind of child study on the part of physicians, psychologists, teachers, and parents, because child growth under these conditions would be quite spontaneous and along natural interest lines.

The last phase of Montessori collective work is seen as a kind of flowering. After children learn how to live together, after they have worked out intellectual problems together, they are suddenly discovered as being very kindly disposed toward each other. It is as if the ultimate development of co-operation were the elimination of war.

It is not necessary to say to a group of Montessori children, "Be good." They could not be otherwise than good.

PICCOLA—LITTLE HOME MAKER

The Helpfulness of the Montessori Child

THE visitor to a Montessori school in Rome is faced by an anomaly.

Piccola, the emotional, eager little Italian girl of five years, who is more difficult to control at home than even the average American child, is seen to be a self-controlled, useful member of a child republic. Piccola's first work of the morning is to find her own pink apron that hangs on a peg on the wall, and button herself into it with patient perseverance. If the younger children have difficulty putting on their aprons, Piccola will patiently help them. Her next activity is, also, along lines of helpfulness. She looks about the wide spaces of the big room, where low white tables and chairs, growing ivy plants, and plain gray wall make a beautiful color scheme, to determine if there is anything she,—wee Piccola, —may do to help this beauty. Ah, Piccola sees a speck of dust in one corner of the white stone floor. Darting to the outer room, where the children remove and hang their wraps and wash their hands before school, Piccola seizes a red broom that is just the right length for her chubby arms to handle easily and a shining little tin dust-pan. Hastening back, she brushes up the dust. Then she waters the ivy with a small green watering pot, fetches a white basin and a little white scrubbing brush, and slops gayly in an energetic attempt to wash off the tables. Last, she takes some of the soft green and gray rugs that the children use for working on when they sit on the floor, and beats them in the garden with much energy.

The other children have come, now, and having selected their materials from the white cupboards that line the wall, are busily at work. Piccola, too, is busy, piling pink blocks in orderly fashion, one upon the other. Her active mind is busy, though, along another line as well; she watches the other little ones furtively to see if there is anything which she can do to help them. Bruno drops his color spools; Piccola runs to help him gather them up in his apron. Little Brother tumbles down in a trip from his table to the material cupboard; Piccola helps him to balance himself again on his fat legs, and, winding two tender little brown arms about him, she steers him in safety on his way.

The hour for the midday luncheon comes. Piccola daintily helps to spread the white luncheon cloths, to lay the spoons in regular order at each child's place, to sort and place the bright baskets in which the children have brought their sandwiches and fruit. Not until all the others are served does Piccola slip into her own empty place and partake of her own luncheon.

Piccola's mother marvels at the change that has been wrought in Piccola by a few months in the Montessori House of the Children. She reports her observations to the Montessori directress who has Piccola's education in charge.

" Piccola dusts the home now, without my bidding.

" She picks up her dolls and her toys when she has finished playing with them.

" She helps me lay the table for the noon meal.

" How did you teach these things to my wayward little Piccola, Signorina? "

It is the query of the American mother who

finds her little one who has spent a day in a good Montessori school more helpful in the home than before.

She also asks herself:

"How may I teach helpfulness to my child?"

Dr. Montessori has discovered for us the marvel that to bring helpfulness to a very little child is not so much a matter of teaching as of fostering. She shows us the instinct to help which manifests itself in the very little child which we must detect, watch, and foster until we form a *habit* of *usefulness* in children. After all, to be useful to oneself and to others is the greatest value of education for life. Dr. Montessori puts this education for utility on a very high plane.

The mother who carefully observes and analyzes all the acts of the child of two and a half or three years of age will discover that the baby has a great desire to be busy, continually, and in imitation of his mother's busy-ness about the home. He handles with the greatest eagerness and interest his shoes, his father's neckties, his mother's brush and comb, the family silver, the kitchen utensils, the door latches and knobs, the window fastenings. He is more interested in the tools of grown-up housekeeping than he is in his toys. Why is this?

A baby of twenty months spent an entire morning collecting all the shoes he could find in his mother's room and carrying them about from one room to another. He climbed up in a chair and pulled a button hook off a dressing table. His mother substituted his dolls, his rubber toys, a ball for these, but the baby refused them. Finally his mother snatched away the huge boot of his father's, which he was lovingly tugging about from room to room and slapped his hands because he cried at giving it up. The little man cried again, and struggled against the brutal force of his mother, who held him tightly in her lap and changed his shoes for going out in the afternoon. Again his hands were slapped.

The baby had not been in the least naughty. He wanted to learn how to button his own shoes and his mother couldn't understand this longing which he had to express in action, having no words with which to explain himself.

Nearly all the instincts of babyhood are *right*

instincts, leading to good conduct. The child's first longing is to be able to fit himself to his environment, and this means that he must learn to handle those objects and do those things which he sees his family doing. The average American child grows up rather helpless and useless when it comes to making social adjustments, because we continually interfere with his first attempts to be useful. We do for him those acts of utility which he should learn himself, very early, while he is still interested in them.

It is undoubtedly less time-taking to put on a small boy's shoes, button and lace them for him, button his under and outer clothes, to tie his necktie, and put on his rubbers, than to slowly and patiently teach him to dress himself. To bathe a child and brush and comb his hair is simpler than to allow the baby to splash in water and revel in soapsuds, as he must in learning the intricate movements necessary for keeping himself tidy. We wish to preserve, also, the immaculate order of our neat bathrooms.

We like to open and close doors for the toddler; it is our privilege of service, we feel. We prefer to lay the table ourselves, and keep our spotless kitchens free of child finger marks. What about the baby, though, who finds his attempts to make himself useful thwarted at every turn until he forms the habit of being waited on? This is a wrecking habit for childhood; it is, also, a habit that leads to our present extravagantly high cost of adult living. The little child who expects to be continually waited on is going to grow up into a man or woman who will expect to be waited on through life. Service is what doubles the grocer's, the butcher's, the landlord's, the shop-keeper's bills.

The useful helpfulness of the Montessori-trained child is easily explained.

The Montessori schoolroom is so planned that there is nothing which a child can hurt and a good deal that he can help by his first clumsy, baby attempts to be useful to himself and to others with his hands. The children are free to move about as much as they like, changing the position of the light little chairs and tables, opening and closing the doors that lead into the garden, unrolling and then rolling up again the rugs, putting away the didactic materials in the cupboards after they are through with them, washing the tables and blackboards, caring for plants and animals, and carrying on countless other activities that bring about hand and eye training.

The children learn, also, all the intricate activities involved in the care of their bodies. They wash their faces and hands, brush their hair, clean their finger nails, black their shoes, put on and take off their aprons. The dressing frames that are included in the Montessori didactic materials include all the different fastenings of a child's clothing; buttoning on red flannel, buttoning on leather, buttoning on drill with tapes, lacing on cloth and on leather, fastening hooks and eyes and snaps, and tying bow knots.

It is quite amazing to see the eagerness with which the Montessori children attack these very universal activities of everyday life. The skill they obtain in them proves the truth of Dr. Montessori's words:

" We habitually *serve* children. This is not only an act of servility toward them, but it is dangerous because it tends to suffocate their useful, spontaneous activity. We are inclined to believe that children are like puppets, and we wash them and feed them as if they were dolls. We do not stop to think that the child who does not do, does not know how to do.

"Our duty toward children is, in every case, that of helping them to make a conquest of such *useful* acts as nature intended man to perform for himself. The mother who feeds her child without making the slightest effort to teach him to hold and use a spoon for himself is not a good mother. She offends the fundamental, human dignity of her son,—she treats him as if he were a doll. Instead, he is a *man*, confided for a time by nature to her care."

There are certain phases of the Montessori method which a mother cannot apply in her home because she has not the preliminary training and the necessary teaching skill. There is not a single activity of the Montessori training for personal and community usefulness of the individual as carried out in the Montessori school that may not be practiced in any home. The Montessori schoolroom is a working duplicate of the best conditions which should exist in every home where there is a baby. It is significant that nations have been aroused by the education miracles wrought in the Roman Children's Houses. What, pray, is the matter with the American children's houses?

The home is a big workshop for turning out child cosmopolites, small world citizens who will grow up into useful men and women. In the home the child may learn how to care for his body, how to care for pets, plants, and all the *things* that combine to fill the tool box of everyday living. Here the child may learn that consideration for others which will help him to be kind, quiet, unselfish, and polite. Here, also, he may take a small part in the care of the big human family in preparing food, laying the table, learning household cleanliness and household order. The child instinct to fetch and carry, which shows itself very early in the life of the baby, may be turned into channels of usefulness if the child is taught to happily wait on himself and others.

Much emphasis has been laid upon the didactic apparatus of Montessori which has for its aim the development of the several intellectual processes. Considering these appliances for direct stimulation and perfection of mental activity only, the casual student of Montessori says that the system is barren, that it takes into account none of the emotional activities of the child, that it eliminates educational play from the life of the little one.

As a matter of fact, the play instincts of the child are so carefully met by Dr. Montessori that they blossom into usefulness. Dr. Montessori knows more about the spontaneous play of the child from two and a half years to six than we do. She sees that his play instincts are all, at first, a struggling to be like his elders, to do the same utilitarian things that he sees them do, to imitate on a child plane the work of his mother in the home or his father in the industrial world. With this understanding of the possibilities of child play for developing into future usefulness, Dr. Montessori supplies children with those tools of play which turn child play into exercises of helpfulness.

In the Trionfale School at Rome the free play of the children has been especially safeguarded. The toddlers utilize their instinct to fetch and carry objects by loading, trundling, and unloading the specially built, stout little wheelbarrows provided for them. Very soon this play blossoms into the desire to fetch and carry with some more useful object in view. The children begin to show great skill in removing and replacing their materials from the school cupboards and putting them back in an orderly fashion. They attain perfect muscular control in laying the tables for luncheon and serving the food daintily. In one corner of a sunlit room at Trionfale there is a fascinating little *salon*. Soft rugs of small size, diminutive green wicker easy-chairs, sofa, and round tea table, books of colored pictures and large dolls' dishes make it possible for the children to " play house " under ideal conditions. They learn through their play a sweet kind of hospitality, and the little school " drawing-room " of Montessori stands for a necessary development of the social instinct in children which is important.

Dr. Montessori suggests to us those playthings and play activities which will lead our children into the art of being helpful and, which is much more vital, will start in them habits of wanting to be helpful. Her scheme of play is possible of adapting to almost any home, and it has for its basis the instinctive longing of every child to be useful through his play.

A playroom should be a place, as Dr. Montessori expresses it, where the children may amuse themselves with games, stories, possibly music, and the furnishing should be done with as much taste as in the sitting-room of the adult members of the family. Small tables, a sofa, and armchairs of child size, one or two casts, copies of masterpieces of art, and vases or bowls in which the children may arrange flowers should be included. There should be many picture books, blocks, dolls, and, if possible, a musical instrument of some kind in the nursery. Dr. Montessori suggests a piano or harp of small dimensions. An important play-room accessory is a low cupboard, with drawers in which the children may keep their completed drawings, paper dolls, scrap pictures, and any precious collection of outside material such as seeds, leaves, twigs, or pebbles which they long to keep and use in their play. Half of this cupboard should consist of shelves for bowls, plates, napkins, doilies, spoons, knives, forks, a tray and tumblers for the children to use in preparing and serving their luncheon or in entertaining their friends. Stout pottery of quaint shapes and exquisite gay coloring may be obtained now. It is much more attractive to the child of three and four years than inadequate, tiny sets of dolls' dishes. At least the necessary bowl, plate, pitcher, and mug for serving the nursery supper should be supplied and the toddler taught to serve and feed himself at a very early age.

The child should have a little broom and dustpan and scrubbing brush. He should have a low, painted washstand with a basin, soap, and nailbrush. He should be taught how to turn on and off a water tap, filling a small pitcher, pail, or basin, and carrying it, full, without spilling. He should have low hooks for hanging his clothing for outdoor wear. Both small boys and girls should have bright little aprons, not so much for purposes of cleanliness, although this is important, as to inspire them to the feeling that work is dignified and needs to be set apart by a uniform of service.

Dr. Montessori urges that those toys which we buy be selected having in mind helping the child to be an actor in a little drama of home life. A plaything, she feels, should be a work thing, capable of bringing a life activity down to the primitive plane of the child's thinking.

Our toy shops offer us now a very wide variety of such educational toys from which to choose. We may find large dolls, modeled from life, and

wearing clothes similar to children and requiring
the same muscular co-ordination in fastening and
unfastening. There is large furniture for these
dolls, built on good lines and teaching a little girl
to make a bed neatly and keep the doll's bureau
drawers in order. There are good-sized washing
sets, including tubs, basket, lines, clothespins,
ironing board, and sad irons; we find very complete dolls' houses, sewing materials with dolls'
patterns and small sewing machines, kitchens
where the child can pretend to cook, complete sets
of cooking utensils, and lifelike toy animals.

These toys Dr. Montessori urges us to use, realizing that the child's deepest play impulse is to
dramatize in the theater of the home playroom
the everyday utilitarian occupations of the race.

MARIO'S PLAYS

Montessori and the Child's Imagination

MARIO played a great deal, and I noticed, as I watched him critically, that his play was of a very strongly imaginative kind.

He was one of the youngest of the little ones at the Trionfale Children's House, and it had taken him a rather longer time than it had the other children to gain control of his impulsive hands, his little truant feet, his vagrant-tending mind. During this first period of his Montessori schooling, when his attention was scattering and he found difficulty in making muscular co-ordination and differentiating form and color clearly, he seemed also to have difficulty in amusing himself. His play impulses at this time seemed to be very primitive; he took pleasure in idling in some sunny spot, kitten-like, or he arranged and rearranged the pieces of wicker furniture which filled the *salon* corner of the schoolroom, or he found entertainment in interfering with the work of the other little ones. There seemed to be no element of creativeness or originality in his play.

Presently, however, Mario began to show a steady intellectual development in his work. Through the physical exercises of Montessori, through the rhythmic exercises carried on with music and through exercises of usefulness in keeping himself and the room neat and waiting upon others, he learned an important lesson of muscular co-ordination.

He learned to make his body respond to the command of his brain.

Through the sense exercises in recognizing fine differentiations of color and form and weight and sound and texture, Mario found a clear mental vision. A month before, the hill back of the school had been a blur to his mental vision. Now it was, for him, a clear percept made up of various component parts. He saw it tall, broad, steep, colored in varying tints of green and brown; its outlines were broken for him by the sunshine, the gardens, the red and yellow tiled houses; he could almost smell the sweet perfume from its orchards and vineyards.

The sense-training of the Montessori system had

quickened and clarified the little boy's perceptive faculties.

Following side by side with Mario's new mental development came as marked a development in his play. His play impulses were no longer scattering but had objectivity. He was, in fancy, a steam engine puffing along or the little father of a group of other children.

As he swung himself over the parallel bars in the school yard he felt that he was a famous acrobat entertaining an applauding audience. In a second he slipped into another path of fancy; as he piled stones into a pyramid, he was a great builder. More than this, Mario's newly-found play impulses carried him into a unique plane of idealism. Crouched in a sunny corner of the playground, he was a sleeping seed; slowly and with spontaneous grace the little body rose, arms upstretched, as Mario felt in dreams the growth of root and branch and flower. No one had taught four-year-old Mario the skill of making real these fantasies. How had he taken his way alone into the fertile fields of the imagination?

It has been suggested that the Montessori system does not take into account the stimulating of

the child's imagination. Daily instances of very
original, undirected imaginative play on the part
of Montessori children show a subtle force at work
in the method which results in a spontaneous unfolding of the imagination. The games and plays
which we teach our children in kindergarten and
primary school are carried on by the Montessori-
trained children without adult supervision. Leaving their work, they run to the garden or playground, imitating with great freedom and beauty
of imagination the activities of the gardener, the
baker, the artisan, the street vender, and the traveling musician. They even impersonate in a more
idealistic way, playing, as did little Mario, that
they are birds and flowers.

This natural expression of imagination in very
young children is an important development of the
method, and a suggestive one.

We are all familiar with the timid, shrinking
little child in the center of a game circle who
doesn't want to be a chickadee, but who is urged
by the teacher in charge of the circle. The child
persists in her disinclination; she is overawed by
so large a ring of spectators; it is possible that
she has never seen a chickadee. The teacher, also,

persists. She goes to the child and tries to teach her the motions of bird flight, but the child sees only an adult running about and waving her arms in an unusual way. She does not connect the spectacle in any way with the free flight of a bird, and when she does take courage and tries to follow the directions of her teacher, the little one is not giving expression to her own mental image, but is endeavoring to imitate a rather ungainly adult.

Is this play of the imaginative type?

It would seem as if we have lost sight of the real character of this elusive, subtle, unexplainable fruition of the mental faculties, the imagination. It is the unforeseen mind power which makes poets and painters and sculptors and conquerors. It is a mind vision which sees success beyond defeat, worth hidden in rags, and good blossoming out of evil. It makes us hear the piping of Pan as the wind blows the reeds beside the river; it promises us a pot of gold if we can build ourselves a rainbow bridge across every cloud of despair; it shows us the lineaments of God in the guise of sorrow and poverty.

Imagination in the child finds varied expressions. There are a great many instances where a child who is lonely and longs for companionship sees and holds daily intercourse with an invisible playmate whom he can describe with great accuracy of detail. In the majority of cases this invisible playmate in disposition, appearance, and tastes is unlike any member of the family or any friend of the child's. Where did the child find this fancy?

A child has the power of a seer to develop the unknown potentialities in apparently dead things. This dry brown leaf, frost-killed of the sap of life, is, in the child's fancy, a gnome, jumping along in the path in front of him to warn the birds of the coming of winter. An acorn is a golden goblet brimming with fairy nectar; a hollow tree is a magic place in which to set up a domicile. No one schooled the child in these tricks of thought. How did he find them?

Dr. Montessori explains the growth of child imagination.

The child is born with a certain defined mental equipment. He has instincts, inherited memories they might be called, and he struggles to feed these instincts. He has capacities for acquiring good or bad habits very early. He has a race-old longing to gain knowledge by means of his senses.

Our part in the education of the child is to study his instinctive activities, giving them opportunities for free expression where they are important for the child's best mental development. A child likes to play in the dirt because his ancestors lived in caves and tilled the soil; it is necessary for the child's best development that he play in sand and model in clay and plant little gardens. A child instinctively fights because his ancestors survived only by warfare; this child instinct we must inhibit.

We must establish good habits in a child early. We must help him, through various sense exercises, to gain clear percepts of his environment. We must try not to force our adult view-point upon the child, but endeavor to establish in him a habit of independent self-active thought.

Then, after we have strengthened the general intellectual processes of the child mind, Dr. Montessori points to us a miracle. Dovetailing instinct and habit and perception, the child intellect begins to build. Clear percepts become concepts; mental images become ideals, imagination appears, building from the clay of everyday-mind stuff a golden castle of dreams.

Imagination cannot be taught. It can scarcely be defined. It can never be prescribed and trained. It is that flowering of the mind processes by means of which a bit of brown sod appears tinted with light and color to the artist, full of potentialities of growth to the gardener, smells of home to the wanderer. If the three types of minds, as children, had been told that a similar piece of sod was a blanket for the sleeping seeds, one questions if it would have been gilded for them in adult life with this glow of individual fancy. On the contrary, the painter has been trained to see color, the gardener has experienced the cultivation of life in the earth, the home lover's hungry senses grasped the memory of former sense stimuli.

Dr. Montessori tells us that the imagination develops variously in different individuals. There may be a child who will never be able to pierce the veil of reality and find his way into the court of fantasy. There will be also the child who develops a seerlike quality of idealism. He moves in a world of blissful unrealities; he sees angels' wings in the clouds and angels' eyes in the stars. Our part in the education of little children is to build the tower for a possible poising of the child's wings of fancy. Then we will wait hopefully for the wonder flight.

The various parts of the didactic apparatus of Montessori presented to a child in their proper relation to his stage of mental growth have a definite place in strengthening the mental processes which lie at the basis of imagination.

We are so unaccustomed to offering any sort of mind food to the child of two and a half or three that we have allowed the little child to go mind hungry. At this early stage of a child's development the right kind of mental training will lay a foundation for the constructive and intellectual processes of imagination and reasoning.

The child of two and three years of age is at the sensory-motor stage of mind development. He longs for experiences which he can turn into action; his mind craves ideas which will express themselves in useful muscular co-ordination and the ability to adjust himself to his environment. To put into a child's hands the materials for this sensory-motor education early is not to overtax his mind; instead, it satisfies his very important mind hunger.

The didactic materials of Montessori that supply this sensory-motor need of the very young child and should be presented early include the various dressing frames, the solid insets, the sound boxes, the blocks of the tower, the broad stair and the long stair, the latter without the use of the sandpaper numerals. As soon as the little one has made his own the muscular co-ordination and ideas of form in relation to size involved in this material and has begun to find the will power to correct his own mistakes, other home activities involving these mental faculties should be added to the use of the Montessori apparatus. The child may dress, undress, bathe himself, dress and undress a doll, build with large blocks, sort various objects of different shapes and sizes, as seeds, nuts, spools, button molds; handle and learn the uses of the furnishings and equipment of the home: toilet utensils, brush, broom, duster, dustpan, kitchen appliances, and the like; he should receive simple ear-training in discriminating different bell tones, high and low, loud and soft notes played on the piano, and hear good models of speech, both in diction and modulation.

At the age of three to four years, the sensory element in the child's mental life is even more prominent, but it is separated a little from motor activities. If the child has had adequate training, he has obtained a large degree of muscular control; he can handle objects without breaking them, he can run without falling down, he can minister to his own bodily needs. Now his mind is hungry for sense images. He wishes to study his environment with the aim of securing a series of definite mind pictures. Ideas are to be stored in the workshop of the child mind for future use in building the power of constructive imagination.

The Montessori didactic apparatus suited to this ideo-sensory stage of the child's development includes the color spools, the geometric insets, the baric sense tablets, the sandpaper boards, and the textiles. The sense-training involved in the child's use of these should be applied in various ways: finding and matching home and outdoor colors, noting the size, shape, and form of various everyday objects, block building with an idea of form, cutting form to line with blunt-pointed scissors, clay-modeling, and constructive sand-play.

The child from four years to five shows a dawning of the constructive imagination. The spool with which he played like a kitten in baby days

has new potentialities in his eyes. Having learned
that it is wooden, round, and will roll, and having
made a mental comparison of it with the wheel of
his toy cart, which is also wooden, round, and
will roll, he calls the spool a wheel. This is a very
important break in the child's mental life. It
demonstrates to us that the child now has ideas
in the abstract. Dr. Montessori meets this with
those of her didactic appliances, which will lead
a child by natural, easy steps from objective to
abstract thinking. She strengthens the sensory
life of the child and guides him toward a grasp
of the symbols of thought. Those parts of the
didactic apparatus which should be presented at
this point to the child are the long stair, with the
sandpaper letters, and the various arithmetic exercises to be had with the rods; the counting boxes
and frame, the sandpaper letters, the movable
alphabet, and the drawing tablets.

Now, the child shows individualistic thinking.
The direct mental training of Montessori has built
a solid foundation for the growth and unfolding
of the imagination. Our place is to watch for
the special trend of his mind development and help
this as far as lies in our power.

Does the child show special interest in the symbols and combinations of number? We should help him to play store, provide him with numerical games, give him a chance to spend and account for a weekly allowance, do home errands, use a tool box, construct cardboard toys, and learn any other possible application of number in its relation to life. Does he make a quick mastery of the symbols of language? We should transfer him as quickly as possible into simple reading books, offering him a great variety of these, that he may feed his imagination with good stories.

It has been said that the average American child exhausts the possibilities of the Montessori apparatus at the age of five years. Of course he does. Dr. Montessori planned it as a means of lighting the flame, touching the torch, opening the switch.

With a marvelous completeness it does this. Our part lies in keeping the flame burning, guiding the express train of the child mind into the higher places of reason, imagination, and personal achievement.

THE GREAT SILENCE

Montessori Development of Repose

It was an amazing fact, but a significant one, that four-year-old Joanina had never been allowed to *feel herself*.

As she lay in her carved-wood cradle, a bundle of cooing, pink delight, she felt for her toes, that she might assure herself of her own identity as represented in those wriggling lumps of flesh. But Joanina's mother bound the little limbs in swaddling bands and the *bambino* lost her toes temporarily. When she was a bit older, and was allowed to bask, kitten-like, on a rug in the garden path, she was charmed to hold her flower-like baby hands up to the light, watching the Roman sunshine trickle through outstretched fingers as she tried to count them. But, always, her emotional, kindly intentioned *madre* would toss a bright-colored ball into the reaching hands or, bending over the baby, would play pat-a-cake with her, or she would suggest a romp up and down the

garden. Her self-imposed quiet was always interrupted by her mother's unrest.

As Joanina grew to a slim little girl of Italy,
whose great, wistful brown eyes reflected a large
curiosity and awe at the surprises of the world
in which she found herself, she was daily surrounded by forces that drew her away from herself. Her home was full of glaring colored pictures hung on vividly dyed wall paper. Her
mother and father talked together in high-pitched,
shrill voices, and through the wide casement windows came the harsh sounds of traveling street
musicians and brawling venders. Always, as a
treat on Sunday or a *festa*, Joanina was taken to
see a procession or to a band concert in one of
the parks. The crowded, hot stone streets, the
noisy cracking of the cab-drivers' whips, the struggle to make her own short legs keep up with the
longer steps of the *madre*, wearied and excited the
little maid.

But she grew accustomed to noise and boister-
ousness in her days; she grew to expect them as
well. Then she came to depend upon *outside*
forces for keeping the motor of her baby spirit
going. She begged for new toys, exhausting

quickly the pleasure to be found in old playthings. She asked for new frocks, aping the vanity of her mother and the other women she saw on the *Corso* on feast days. She allowed her child playmates to plan her games. She cried to be taken into the turbid streets. From a placid, reposeful baby, Joanina developed into a restless, passionate, distraction-seeking little girl. Germs of discontent, disquiet, hysteria were planted in her child soul.

When Joanina found herself one morning in the Trionfale Children's House, she experienced an unconscious feeling of peace. The very wide spaces of the two rooms where the little ones busily and happily worked; the cool gray walls unbroken in their sweep save by a blue and white terra-cotta bas-relief here and there; the plain brown linen curtains that softened and toned the yellow sunlight and rippled with a flower-scented breeze— these helped to make Joanina's peace. Dropping into one of the little white chairs, she looked about her with eyes that again melted into the calm wonder of her babyhood. She could not have explained it, but there was already at home in her life a new, quiet repose.

Surrounding her was a child republic that

opened its heart to her. Some of the children, in groups, were sorting and grading with quiet skill scores of the silk-wound color spools. Others, alone, were testing their knowledge of dimension and form with the solid and geometric insets. In a corner, a determined baby was trying to button the apron of another baby. All were entertained, yet no one was entertaining them. They were making their own content.

Without warning, the directress turned from the child whom she had been giving a lesson in numbers with the counting case, moved to the front of the room, and wrote upon the blackboard one word, Silence. Then she waited, herself silent and facing the little ones. Joanina, too, waited. She did not understand; she was curious.

The children, recognizing the written word, one by one laid down their work, dropped into positions of quiet repose, their eyes closed. Some laid their heads upon their folded arms. The room became so hushed that such faint sounds as the low ticking of the clock, the hum of a buzzing fly, the gentle rise and fall of breathing, became vibrant. The children's faces were full of calm joy, their bodies were completely motionless. They

had gone away from their small republic of work
and play for a space. Who could tell where they
were? Each child was feeling himself; for the
time being he was listening to the call of his own
personality.

Joanina, interested in the game of silence, closed
her eyes. She folded her restless fingers. She
waited, rapt, immobile as a little chiseled cherub.
It was perhaps the first time in her four years'
apprenticeship to Life that she had been given an
opportunity to listen to her own heart throbs, feel
the grip of her own personality. The experience
was satisfying to her. She heard and felt a great
many inner voices and mental forces that she had
never listened to or obeyed before. She heard the
voices of happiness in her new, peaceful environment and love for the other children and joy at
the complete freedom that surrounded her. She
felt the impulse to *do* and *learn* as she had seen
the other children doing and learning.

For several minutes, the silence held the children
in its spell. Then, out of the stillness the whispered voice of the directress floated. As a singing
wind of a far-away forest, a mountain echo, or the
low voice of a mother as it first makes itself audi-

ble to a new-born babe, came the voice: " Joanina."

The little girl opened her eyes, meeting the smiling ones of the directress, who made a gesture indicating that Joanina should go to her quietly. Poised on tiptoe, Joanina crossed the room noiselessly, threw herself into the outstretched arms of the directress.

" Mario, Otello," softly the other children were called until all had, as silently as Joanina, left their places and surrounded the directress. Their eyes shone, their faces glowed as if they had been refreshed by an elixir bath. Yet the Montessori silence game which had brought about this inspiration and refreshing in the life of soul-starved little Joanina might have been a part of her home life.

Your child needs it; *you* need it.

There is, perhaps, no more significant phase of the Montessori system of education than the calm, quiet habit of self-contemplation aroused by the game of silence. The self-control, the poise, the power of long concentration that one sees in the Montessori children at Rome amazes the world. They are completely lacking in self-consciousness; they ask for help in their work only when it is absolutely necessary; they are *sure* of themselves.

In writing about the game of silence, it has been suggested that the game has an hypnotic quality; that the calm, beautifully poised directress imposes her own personality upon the children, controls them as the hypnotist controls his subject. This is not true. As the didactic materials furnish the right means for the child's mental development, so the opportunity given by the game of silence makes possible the child's moral and spiritual development. It gives him a chance to listen to the " still, small voice " that is a speaking voice in childhood but which is drowned by the babel of world tongues that we allow to make our song of life in adult years.

The story of Joanina, the little Roman girl, is retold in almost every American home. As we, ourselves, depend upon public opinion, outside amusements, entertaining friends, the judgment of the press, the fashions of the day for filling our lives, so we make our children, also, dependent upon similar forces for forming their characters. We surround children with gossip, we teach them to depend upon excitement for their pleasure; we build their ideals of conduct upon what the world will think instead of what their conscience dictates. We make of our little ones modern Babes in the Woods who lose themselves in a forest of bewildering, overgrown paths. We give them no chance to blaze their own trails.

What is the application to the American home of the Montessori game of silence?

It begins with the American mother who must cultivate a habit of quiet self-contemplation. She must be able to shut out the world as did the stoics, listening to the good voice of her own soul. It means, also, that she will be less dependent upon her environment for her daily thinking and happiness and more adept at creating her own joys. We are very restless, to-day, discontented unless we are surrounded by friends or obsessed by passion of some sort, or we must go somewhere. We will try to slip back into the simple living of our great-grandmothers, who had resources in themselves and could be radiantly happy, pottering over the lavender in their gardens or reading their Bibles in the candlelight of some long-ago evening —alone.

The mother who cultivates in herself a habit of repose will have reposeful children.

The game of silence, as it may be put into practice in the training of children, begins with ear-training. Shut out harsh sounds from the home where there are little children. To command a child in a loud voice often results in disobedience; it makes him mentally deaf for the time being. He does not hear what is said to him; it dulls his senses. We all know how the memory of some gentle voice that either sang or spoke to us in childhood comes back to us, now, as a forceful memory. It was the softness of that voice that made the lasting record in our minds.

Often a mother may whisper a sentence to a child, or call softly from different parts of the house, asking the little one to locate her by the sense of hearing. This will quicken and cultivate the child's power to listen and concentrate upon the use of one sense. And we should eliminate all unnecessary noises from our homes; the slamming of doors, the crashing of dishes, harsh popular music, and crude songs.

As the children's sense of hearing is refined, we will lead them to listen to the very small sounds in the world about them, the soft breathing of the sleeping baby, the far-away ticking of a clock, the hum of insects, distant footsteps, the patter of rain, the song of the wind.

Then when this fine power of listening has been cultivated, we may introduce the game of silence itself. The mother may show the child that she is able to sit quietly, immobile, relaxed for a short period of time—only thinking. Then the little ones may be encouraged to attempt the game, waiting in perfect silence, with closed eyes, until mother calls them in a soft whisper to " come back " to the world again. To darken the room a little during the game adds to its power. Gradually the periods of the silence may be lengthened, and results will show in the child's life in greater control, quiet, and life balance. In this repose and silence, Dr. Montessori tells us, both adults and children gather strength and newness of life.

A little maid of three had been having her first birthday party. Light and music and romping games and many gifts had filled the afternoon with unexperienced delights for the child. She was trembling with delight, on tiptoe with excitement when the children marched out to the dining-room and were seated about the beautifully laid, rose-strewn table. At a signal the curtains were drawn and the children were told to be silent and close their eyes for a space. There was a vibrant hush, a space of time passed, then one child after another raised her head and opened her eyes. The room was still darkened, but in the center of the table had been placed the huge, white birthday cake surrounded by a wreath of flowers; the only light was the starry shining of three white candles on the top. The little birthday child looked in wonder. Then she drew a long breath and said in a whisper, " Nearer, my God, to Thee."

No one quite understood the little one. It seemed to have been a vagary, a precocity on her part. It *was* an unusual manifestation, but quite explainable as we grew to realize the inspirational possibilities of the Montessori silence.

When it is not possible, because we are dealing with an isolated child, to put into practice the game of silence as it is used in the Children's Houses, we can still lead the child to know and feel silence. A quiet hour in the twilight after the work and play of the daytime are over, a trip to some still, lovely spot in the woods, a few moments spent in the hushed interior of a church, will remain as reposeful memories in the life of the child. More than repose, even, they may be inspirational, as, shut away from the noise and activity of the world, the child is able to hear the call of his own spirit.

We all know and love Bastien-Lepage's painting of the maid, Jeanne d'Arc, listening to the voices in her garden. The grass dotted with flowers, the bending apple tree, the other homely surroundings of the humble home that were all Jeanne had known, fade away as the voice of the prophetic soul speaks to her; as she sees the vision of herself, the saviour of France.

Jeanne d'Arc was only thirteen when she began to hear the voice of her spirit.

Millet, as a boy, saw nature with his spirit eyes. He showed his father colors playing over the rough sod of his home fields which no one else could see. Rousseau, in boyhood, declared that he was able to converse with his beloved trees and they told him the secrets of their beauty. Samuel was only a very little boy when he heard and interpreted his Master's voice. The boy Christ heard a message that he was able to carry to the doctors.

May we not give our little ones an opportunity to step across the threshold of the present into that great silence which begins life and also ends it, and which is melodious for those who are trained to listen?

THE END

BOOKS ON AND OF SCHOOL PLAYS

By Constance D'Arcy Mackay

HOW TO PRODUCE CHILDREN'S PLAYS

The author is a recognized authority on the production of plays and pageants in the public schools, and combines enthusiastic sympathy with sound, practical instructions. She tells both how to inspire and care for the young actor, how to make costumes, properties, scenery, where to find designs for them, what music to use, etc., etc. She prefaces it all with an interesting historical sketch of the plays-for-children movement, includes elaborate detailed analyses of performances of Browning's *Pied Piper* and Rosetti's *Pageant of the Months,* and concludes with numerous valuable analytical lists of plays for various grades and occasions. $1.20 net (Feb., 1914).

PATRIOTIC PLAYS AND PAGEANTS

PAGEANT OF PATRIOTISM (Outdoor and Indoor Versions):— *Princess Pocahontas, Pilgrim Interlude, Ferry Farm Episode, *George Washington's Fortune, *Daniel Boone: Patriot, Benjamin Franklin Episode, Lincoln Episode, Final Tableau.

HAWTHORNE PAGEANT (for Outdoor or Indoor Production):—Chorus of Spirits of the Old Manse, Prologue by the Muse of Hawthorne, In Witchcraft Days, Dance Interlude, Merrymount, etc.

The portions marked with a star (*) are one-act plays suitable for separate performance. There are full directions for simple costumes, scenes, and staging. 12mo. $1.35 net.

THE HOUSE OF THE HEART

Short plays in verse for children of fourteen or younger:— "The House of the Heart (Morality Play)—"The Enchanted Garden" (Flower Play)—"A Little Pilgrim's Progress" (Morality Play)—"A Pageant of Hours" (To be given Out of Doors)—"On Christmas Eve." "The Princess and the Pixies." "The Christmas Guest" (Miracle Play.), etc. $1.10 net.
"An addition to child drama which has been sorely needed."—*Boston Transcript.*

THE SILVER THREAD

AND OTHER FOLK PLAYS. "The Silver Thread" (Cornish); "The Forest Spring" (Italian); "The Foam Maiden" (Celtic); "Troll Magic" (Norwegian); "The Three Wishes" (French); "A Brewing of Brains" (English); "Siegfried" (German); "The Snow Witch" (Russian). $1.10 net.

HENRY HOLT AND COMPANY
PUBLISHERS   NEW YORK

CPSIA information can be obtained
at www.ICGtesting.com
Printed in the USA
LVHW081057270123
738086LV00008B/180